DRESSINGS
AND MARINADES

D0996104

017835

00735954

DRESSINGS
AND MARINADES

Classic and novel ways to
enliven every dish

HILAIRE WALDEN

APPLE

017835

A QUINTET BOOK

Published by The Apple Press
6 Blundell Street
London N7 9BH

Copyright © 1996 Quintet Publishing Limited.
All rights reserved. No part of this publication
may be reproduced, stored in a retrieval system or
transmitted in any form or by any means,
electronic, mechanical, photocopying, recording
or otherwise, without the permission of the
copyright holder.

ISBN 1-85076-673-8

This book was designed and produced by
Quintet Publishing Limited
6 Blundell Street
London N7 9BH

Creative Director: Richard Dewing
Designer: Ian Hunt
Senior Editor: Laura Sandelson
Editor: Gail Dixon Smith
Photographer: David Armstrong

Typeset in Great Britain by
Central Southern Typesetters, Eastbourne
Manufactured in Singapore by
Eray Scan (Pte) Ltd
Printed in Singapore by
Star Standard Industries (Pte) Lte

CONTENTS

INTRODUCTION

Salad dressings and marinades are both easy ways of making food more exciting and interesting, highlighting its intrinsic flavour, complementing it or giving it new flavour. They can both be flavoured in an almost infinite number of ways using ingredients from around the world.

Salad Dressings

Salad dressings are vital to the success of a salad; they can make it by adding a touch of originality, freshness or distinction, or spoil it by being insipid, inappropriate or overdone. A salad dressing can transform simple ingredients into a special treat, vegetables into an exotic dish.

Try to match the ingredients of a dressing to the salad ingredients. For example, Walnut Dressing (see page 61) blends excellently with a pear and blue cheese salad and adds an extra, complementary flavour and texture; Basil Dressing (see page 43) has a natural affinity to a simple summery salad of sliced, well-flavoured sun-ripened tomatoes.

However good a dressing, do not add so much that the salad ingredients are drowned.

The two most widely used salad dressings are the simple French Dressing (see page 18) and mayonnaise (see page 19). Historically this has been a troublesome sauce to make because unless care is taken when making it, it will curdle or fail to thicken. But now, thanks to blenders and food processors, homemade mayonnaise can be made with greater assurance, and more quickly (see page 19). It is still necessary though, to make sure all the ingredients are at room temperature and not to add the oil too quickly. Unless you have a small blender or food processor bowl, a two egg yolk/300 ml/½pt oil quantity is the minimum that can be made because the blender or processor blades must be covered by the egg yolks

when starting to make the sauce. Should mayonnaise curdle while you are making it, put another egg yolk, at room temperature, in a clean bowl then very gradually add the curdled mixture, whisking constantly.

Many different dressings can be made using a basic French dressing-type mixture or mayonnaise. For example, the character can easily be varied enormously by using different types of oil and vinegars or fruit juices such as lemon, lime and orange, the type of mustard as well, and of course, by adding flavouring ingredients such as herbs, spices, garlic and shallots, producing a vast repertoire of recipes with flavours as diverse as Chinese, Indian, Thai, East meets West, Mexican, Middle Eastern, Italian and Greek.

Try to make a salad dressing about 30 minutes before it is to be used to allow the flavours to develop, although herbs are best not added until the last moment as they can discolour. Whisk French dressing-type dressings again before using. Thin dressings are usually used for leaf salads while thicker dressings are more suitable for mixing with firmer textured ingredients such as potatoes and chicken.

A dressing is usually added to leaf salads, except cabbage, immediately before being served, otherwise the leaves wilt. Cooked vegetables such as potatoes, pasta, pulses and grilled aubergines are usually mixed with the dressing while they are warmed then left to cool, so they absorb the flavours of the dressing. Raw ingredients such as sliced mushrooms are also sometimes left to marinate for a while in the dressing.

Salads are not the only foods that salad dressings can be used with. They can also be served over or with plain grilled, baked and roasted meat, poultry, game, fish and vegetables.

Marinades

Marinades are used on food before cooking to give it flavour, prevent it from drying, and to tenderize meat, game, poultry and, to a lesser degree, fish.

Marinades can be divided into three groups – wet marinades, pastes and dry or spice rubs.

A wet marinade is a well-flavoured liquid in which food is steeped. It will contain an acid such as wine, vinegar, plain yogurt or fruit juice, a little oil and flavouring such as herbs or spices. The amount of oil will depend on how the food is to subsequently be cooked; marinades for grilling usually contain at least 25 per cent oil whereas there will be much less in marinades for casseroles.

There are two main types of wet marinade: uncooked and cooked. Uncooked marinades are used for tender or relatively tender foods such as chicken, pork, fish and vegetables, and cuts of lamb and beef for grilling, frying or roasting. Most marinades made nowadays are uncooked.

Cooked marinades are usually wine-based and are used for red meats and game. Before cooking the marinated food, drain the food and dry it thoroughly otherwise it will not brown. An exception to this rule is food marinated in yogurt. The remaining marinade is often used in the cooking of the dish.

A paste is a thick mixture that is spread in an even layer over food that is to be grilled, roasted or baked. Not only will a paste provide a protective coating during cooking, but when left to marinate, it will penetrate food, giving it additional flavour and tenderizing foods such as meats and fish. During cooking, pastes often develop a crisp crust with a delicious slightly caramelized or smoky-taste.

Dry marinades, or spice rubs, are blends of herbs, usually dried, and spices that are rubbed into meat, poultry, game and fish. The herbs and spices are lightly crushed together in a pestle and mortar (or with the end of a rolling-pin in a bowl). The food should be dried thoroughly first then rubbed with oil before the spice rub is applied. It is then left to marinate before cooking.

Salt is not added to marinades for meats, game, poultry and fish because it draws out their juices.

The container used for marinating should be made from a non-reactive material such as glass and it should not be too large. The longer a food is left in a marinade, the more flavour it will absorb and the greater the tenderizing effect; and the flavour of foods at room temperature will develop twice as fast as those in the refrigerator. Slashing the food will hasten penetration of the marinade so reducing the marinating time. The smaller the piece of food and the more delicate its texture, generally the shorter the marinating time. The food should be completely covered by the marinade and stirred or turned during the marinating time.

Foods that are left in the refrigerator to marinate should be returned to room temperature about 30 minutes before cooking, depending on the size of the food and the length of time refrigerated.

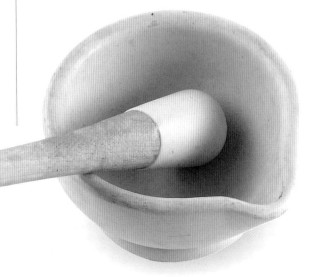

Ingredients for Salad Dressings

EGGS – some eggs have been shown to contain salmonella so the elderly, young, babies, pregnant women and people with poor immune defence systems are advised not to eat raw or lightly cooked eggs.

GARLIC – garlic is nearly always used raw in dressings and marinades, so it really is important that firm cloves that are as fresh as possible are used. Ideally, the cloves should not have green sprouts growing out of their tops, but if they do, be sure to remove all of the sprout as it tastes bitter.

Buy garlic that feels firm, is shiny with the paper skin still attached, not peeling off in flakes. Store garlic in a cool, dark, airy place.

The intensity of the garlic flavour varies according to how the cloves are prepared. For salad dressings, it is best to crush the cloves with a small pinch of salt because, not only does chopping give a harsher flavour than crushing them, but many people do not like to bite on small pieces of raw garlic.

Another way to add a mild garlic flavour to a salad dressing is to roast the cloves (see page 70).

To give a mild garlic flavour to a salad, the salad bowl can be rubbed with a cut clove of garlic.

HERBS – all the recipes in this book have been made using fresh herbs, except where dried ones are mentioned as in the spice rubs. With the exception of the rubs, I never use dried herbs. If I do not have the fresh herb I want growing in my garden, either in the ground or in a pot, in a window box or in a pot on the windowsill (a surprising number of herbs can be grown successfully in tubs, window boxes and pots on windowsills) and I am unable to buy fresh herbs, I buy frozen or freeze-dried herbs, which most supermarkets now stock. Many supermarkets and greengrocers also sell herbs growing in pots.

Store fresh herbs in "stay-fresh" bags in the refrigerator.

Fresh herbs can vary quite considerably in flavour, so it is important to taste each batch you are using and adjust the amount you use as necessary.

OILS – oils are the foundation of most salad dressings and are an important addition to marinades because they add flavour to the food being marinated, lubricate it and keep it moist during cooking (see pages 10–11).

PEPPER – along with salt, pepper, usually black, is the common seasoning for salad dressings. White pepper may be used where dark specks of black pepper would spoil the appearance of a recipe.

To give your salad dressings the best flavour use freshly ground peppercorns rather than ground pepper as this is too fine and powdery and lacks the fresh piquancy of freshly ground corns.

SALT – many experienced cooks prefer to use sea salt or other coarse salts, believing their flavour to be superior to ordinary table salt, but at a recent tasting of a wide selection of different salts, involving top British food writers and chefs, the salt that came out on top was common table salt!

SOY SAUCE – now used not only in Chinese and Japanese cooking, but also in other recipes to add depth to the flavour, as well as a characteristic taste.

Light Soy Sauce – this is light in colour but it has a full flavour and is more salty than dark soy sauce. In Chinese shops light soy sauce is known as Superior Soy. It is the sauce that is generally used for cooking; the word "light" may not always be included.

Dark Soy Sauce – this is matured for longer than light soy sauce so has a darker colour. Its flavour is slightly stronger than light soy sauce and it is slightly thicker. It is known as Soy Superior Sauce in Chinese grocers, and is the one most often sold there. Its most common use is in dipping sauces.

SPICES – for the best flavour, use freshly ground spices rather than ready ground ones. To get the maximum flavour from the whole spices, before grinding them, heat them gently in a heated heavy frying pan until they smell fragrant.

Because the flavour of spices deteriorates with age, buy spices in small amounts that you will use quickly; if you have any for more than 6 months, throw them away. Keep the spices in a cool, dark, dry place.

SZECHUAN PEPPERCORNS – reddish brown colour and a sharp, mildly spicy flavour that has a hint of lavender. Szechuan peppercorns do not come from the same family as white, black and green peppercorns and do not have the same "hotness". Szechuan peppercorns are usually dry roasted and ground before using to bring out their full flavour.

VINEGAR – vinegar is the second most important ingredient in salad dressings and marinades, after oil. Vinegar is important in both dressings and marinades for adding flavour and piquancy, and in dressings it is important for forming an emulsion with the oil, so thickening the sauce, while in marinades it tenderizes meat, poultry, game and fish (see pages 13–15).

Oils

Oils flavoured with aromatics such as herbs and spices are useful for instantly adding flavour to a dressing. All oils should be kept in a cool, dark place. Mild oils should then keep fresh for 6–9 months; olive oils, nut oils and sesame oil should be used within 4–6 months, the better the quality of an olive oil, the more quickly it should be used.

Olive Oil – there is now a burgeoning range of olive oils of different styles and qualities. The descending order of quality, purity, intensity of flavour and price of the grades is:

EXTRA VIRGIN OLIVE OIL – from the first pressing of the olives. This has the lowest acidity and the most rounded flavour. Commercially produced extra virgin oils are blended from oils of differing character and quality and will always taste the same. Extra virgin oils from estates, farms and village co-operatives have their own individual characters and, as they are unblended, will vary from year to year in the same way as wine. These oils are used in salads and marinades where a rich olive taste is wanted, or when only small quantitites of oil are required.

VIRGIN OLIVE OIL – the result of the second pressing of the olives. Virgin olive oils are used for salad dressings where a less pronounced but still discernible olive flavour is required, and more widely in cooking.

SIMPLE OLIVE OIL – or pure olive oil – a blend of virgin olive oil and refined olive oils obtained by chemical extraction. It is used for salad dressings and marinades where the taste of the oil should be barely noticeable.

Within each category, there is a range of flavours. Oils from different countries, areas and producers can range from delicate and grassy to full, heavy and fruity. Spanish oils tend to be lighter than Italian ones, whereas Greek oils are even heavier because the olives are allowed to become very ripe before they are picked.

Colour is not an indication of quality, but a rich dark green oil does indicate a strength of flavour.

CORN OIL – also goes under the name of maize oil. It is quite bland but has a slight smell and taste (which some people find unpleasant) so is more suitable for cooking than making salad dressings.

GRAPESEED OIL – a pale oil with a mild nutty taste. It makes good salad dressings.

PEANUT OIL – also known as ground nut or arachide oil, has a light texture and a pleasant, mild, unobtrusive taste which makes it a good all-purpose oil. In salad dressings and marinades it is useful when the flavour of choice ingredients needs to show through. Peanut oil found in Asian food shops has a stronger taste of peanuts and is more expensive.

SAFFLOWER OIL – a pale, bland oil that is very high in polyunsaturates, which are believed to break down cholesterol. Safflower oil is good for cooking and mild salad dressings.

SESAME OIL – is a thick, rich, golden brown oil made from sesame seeds, which give it a distinctive nutty flavour and aroma. Sesame oil made from toasted seeds is darker and has a richer, toasted flavour so is used in small quantities mixed with milder oils.

SUNFLOWER OIL – lighter than corn oil but slightly more cloying and robustly flavoured than peanut oil, it makes a good, all-purpose oil.

VEGETABLE OIL – is a blend of oils from various vegetable products, such as soya, rapeseed, palm and coconut. (Check individual labels for precise details.) Vegetable oils are usually cooking oils.

WALNUT AND HAZELNUT OILS – have full, rich tastes and aromas so are best used in combination with olive oil or a mild oil. Nut oils are particularly good with bitter salad greens and mushrooms. Nut oils become rancid more quickly than other oils so it is adviseable to buy them in small quantities and it is even more essential to keep them in a cool, dark place.

Flavoured Oils

These are oils that have herbs steeped or soaked in them. They have long been used in Mediterranean, Indian, Chinese and other Asian cooking. It is best to buy flavoured oils that have been commercially prepared because preparing them at home, especially those oils containing garlic and onion, can promote the growth of botulism. Commercially prepared and with the proper preservatives, however, these oils can be considered perfectly safe – and delicious. They should be refrigerated after opening.

A store-bought infused oil can liven up a vinaigrette. Or you can dip dense bread into flavoured oil for an imaginative alternative to butter. Flavoured oil can also provide the perfect complement to pasta, pizza or bruschetta. Flavoured oil can top a baked potato or substitute for butter and milk to make garlicky mashed potatoes. You could also try sautéeing fresh artichoke hearts in an infused oil, or drizzling a little over poached salmon, broiled eggplant, roasted peppers, or other vegetables. A low-fat or non-fat prepared mayonnaise can also be jazzed up with a little infused oil.

Vinegars

Balsamic vinegar – is a special Italian red wine vinegar that has been aged in barrels for a number of years; the longer the maturing the darker the colour, the more intense the sweet-sharp flavour, and the higher the price. Only a few drops of this vinegar are needed when using in dressings, but of the cheaper, though not cheap, commercial balsamic vinegars you will need to use a little more.

Cider vinegar – mild, slightly sweet, apple flavour.

Distilled white vinegar – too strong and dominantly flavoured to use for dressings and marinades.

Flavoured vinegars – such as tarragon, raspberry, garlic or chilli instantly add flavour to a dressing. Flavoured vinegars are very easy to make at home (see pages 14 and 15).

Malt vinegar – this brown vinegar, like distilled vinegar, is unsuitable for salad dressings and marinades.

Rice vinegar – this is made from rice. There are two main types of rice vinegar.

WHITE RICE VINEGAR – is clear with a delicate flavour that has a slight nuance of glutinous rice. It has a low acid content, so is mild, therefore, to give piquancy to a recipe, you will need to add more white rice vinegar than you would white wine vinegar.

BLACK RICE VINEGAR – an inky black Chinese rice vinegar that has a rich, spicy fragrance.

Japanese rice vinegar has a smoother, more mellow, almost sweet taste compared to Chinese rice vinegar, which is sharper.

Sherry vinegar – is made from the grape most used in sherry making and is aged in old sherry casks which give it a unique, rich, sweetish, sherry-like flavour. Like balsamic vinegar, sherry vinegar should be used more like a seasoning than an acidifier.

Wine vinegars – the quality of wine vinegars varies considerably but price is usually a good guide; Orleans wine vinegars are the best but only one company, Martin Pouret, still makes them. Red wine vinegar has a stronger flavour than a white wine vinegar of the same brand.

Flavoured Vinegars

Herb Vinegars

Most culinary herbs can be used to make flavoured vinegars – tarragon, rosemary, thyme, marjoram, parsley, basil, bay, fennel, dill and sage. They can be used either individually or as a mixture.

Use fresh, preferably freshly picked, herbs. Pick herbs in the morning of a dry day, after the dew has disappeared but before the sun is too hot, and select sprigs on which flowers have not formed.

METHOD

Bruise the herbs lightly to release their flavour and pack into a jar or bottle so that it is half-filled. Pour in white or red wine vinegar to fill the jar or bottle and seal tightly with non-reactive tops.

Shake the bottle or jar and leave in a cool dark place for 2–3 weeks, shaking every day.

Strain the vinegar, pressing down well on the herbs. Taste the vinegar to see if the herb flavour is strong enough. If it is not, repeat the process. A fresh herb sprig can be added to the prepared vinegar, if liked.

Garlic Vinegar

MAKES ABOUT 700 ML/1¼ PT

INGREDIENTS

12 plump garlic cloves	garlic cloves for garnish (optional)
700 ml/1¼ pt white wine vinegar	

METHOD

Lightly crush the garlic cloves and put them into a jar or bottle. Pour in the vinegar, cover and shake the jar or bottle. Leave in a cool, dark place for 2–3 weeks.

If the flavour of the vinegar is strong enough, strain it and re-bottle. If liked, thread 2–3 garlic cloves per bottle onto a wooden cocktail stick and add to each bottle.

Herbes de Provence Vinegar

MAKES ABOUT 700 ML/1¼ PT

INGREDIENTS

3 large sprigs of tarragon	4 bay leaves
3 large sprigs of thyme	pinch of fennel seeds
3 sprigs of rosemary	700 ml/1¼ pt white wine vinegar

METHOD

Lightly bruise the herbs then pack into a jar or bottle. Pour in the vinegar and close tightly. Shake the jar or bottle and leave in a cool dark place for 2–3 weeks, shaking the jar or bottle daily.

Strain the vinegar, pressing down well on the herbs. Taste the vinegar to see if the herb flavour is strong enough. If it is not, repeat the process. A fresh herb sprig can be added to the prepared vinegar, if liked.

Fruit Vinegars

MAKES ABOUT 450 ML/16 FL OZ

For a few years fruit vinegars seemed to appear in all manner of recipes, irrespective of whether they really contributed anything beneficial to the dish. Now, thank goodness, moderation and sense have prevailed. Use this vinegar, which has quite a concentrated flavour, to add an interesting fruity flavour to dressings for rich meats such as duck or game and salads containing fruit.

INGREDIENTS

450 g/1 lb fruit such as raspberries, strawberries or blackcurrants	450 ml/16 fl oz white wine vinegar
	50 g/2 oz sugar

METHOD

Put the fruit into a non-metallic bowl or jar, add a little of the vinegar and crush the fruit with the back of a wooden spoon to release the juice. Add the remaining vinegar, cover and leave in a cool place for 1 week, stirring occasionally.

Strain the vinegar into a saucepan, add the sugar and heat gently, stirring until the sugar has dissolved. Bring to the boil. Cool.

Pour the vinegar into a clean bottle, cover and store in a cool, dark place.

Orange Vinegar

MAKES ABOUT 1 L/1¾ PT

INGREDIENTS

3 large oranges	1 small orange
1 l/1¾ pt white wine vinegar	

METHOD

Thinly pare the rind from the 3 large oranges, taking care not to include any white pith. Put the rind into a clean large jar. Cut the 3 oranges in half and squeeze out the juice. Pour into the jar, seal and shake. Leave in a cool, dark place for 3 weeks, shaking the jar occasionally.

Strain the vinegar and re-bottle. Thinly pare some of the rind from the small orange so no pith is included. Cut the rind into thin strips and add 3 strips to each bottle.

CLASSIC
SALAD DRESSINGS

———

Some salad dressings such as French Dressing and Mayonnaise are classics in their own right and can be used with a number of different type of salads whereas others, such as Caesar Salad Dressing and Tuna Mayonnaise are most often associated with particular salads; this does not mean that they cannot be combined with other salad ingredients. Tuna Mayonnaise, which partners *Vitello Tonnato* (cold poached veal) also marries well with boiled eggs, chicken, and crisp green salad leaves.

French Dressing

MAKES 5 TABLESPOONS

French dressing (or vinaigrette to use the French name) is a simple combination of oil, vinegar and seasoning, whisked together until the oil and vinegar have emulsified and the dressing has thickened. The usual proportions of oil to vinegar are about 3–4:1 but this can be varied according to the acidity of the vinegar, how sharp you want the dressing to be and the composition of the salad. Mustard, usually Dijon, is an optional flavouring, usually in the proportion of ½ teaspoon to 3–4 parts oil and 1 part vinegar, but it will also help an emulsion to form. Use whatever type of oil you prefer. The basic dressing, without the optional garlic, will keep for as long as 1 month in a screw-top jar in the refrigerator.

French dressing can be used over a limitless number of salad ingredients.

INGREDIENTS

3–4 tbsp oil

1 tbsp white wine vinegar

½ tsp *Dijon* mustard (optional)

salt and freshly ground black pepper

METHOD

Put all the ingredients into a bowl and whisk together until emulsified and thickened.

Mayonnaise

MAKES 350 ML / 12 FL OZ

INGREDIENTS

**2 egg yolks
(see page 8)**

**about 1 tsp *Dijon*
mustard**

**2 tbsp white wine
vinegar or lemon juice**

300 ml/½ pt oil

**salt and freshly ground
white or black pepper**

The keys to success when making mayonnaise are having all the ingredients at room temperature and adding the oil very slowly, especially at first, and whisking all the time.

Whether you use all olive oil, half olive oil and half a bland oil such as sunflower oil, or all of a bland oil is a matter of personal taste. For extra character, use a proportion of a nut oil. The choice of wine vinegar or lemon juice is also a question of individual taste and the use to which the sauce is to be put.

Homemade mayonnaise can be kept in a covered container in the refrigerator for up to 3 days. If the mayonnaise becomes too thick during this time, stir in a little water to thin it.

METHOD

Put the egg yolks into a bowl and stir in half of the vinegar or lemon juice, and the mustard.

Add the oil, drop by drop, whisking constantly. After about half of the oil has been incorporated the rest can be added slightly more quickly but continue to whisk, until all the oil has been emulsified and the sauce is thick and shiny.

Beat in the remaining vinegar or lemon juice and season to taste; add more mustard, if liked.

Blender Mayonnaise

Put the egg yolks, mustard, seasoning and half of the vinegar or lemon juice into a blender or food processor and mix together briefly at low speed until blended. With the motor running, slowly pour in the oil in a thin, steady stream to make a thick, emulsified sauce. Add the remaining vinegar or lemon juice.

NOTE: when making mayonnaise in a blender or food processor 1 whole egg rather than 2 egg yolks can be used, which will make a lighter sauce.

Caesar Salad Dressing

MAKES ABOUT 225 ML / 8 FL OZ

Now an American classic, Caesar salad was invented in Tijuana, Mexico by Caesar Cardini. During the Prohibition era Americans flooded over the border to his restaurant in search of hard liquor which they were unable to get at home. The salad was later popularized in the New York restaurant Chasens, and is now available across the nation. Needless to say, there are quite a number of versions of the dressing.

INGREDIENTS

3 garlic cloves	about 6 tbsp virgin olive oil
2 egg yolks (see page 8)	50 g/2 oz freshly grated Parmesan cheese
1 tsp Worcestershire sauce	salt and freshly ground black pepper
1 tbsp lemon juice	

METHOD

Mash the garlic with a pinch of salt in a bowl using the end of a rolling-pin. Whisk in the egg yolks, Worcestershire sauce and lemon juice.

Slowly pour in the oil, whisking constantly until well emulsified. Stir in the cheese then season to taste.

Boiled Salad Dressing

MAKES ABOUT 375 ML / 13 FL OZ

This old-fashioned dressing is useful for those who do not like oil. It goes well with shredded celeriac and cabbage, green and vegetable salads, and eggs.

INGREDIENTS

20 g/¾ oz plain flour	175 ml/6 fl oz milk
1 tsp dry mustard powder	2 tbsp melted butter
15 g/½ oz sugar	4 tbsp white wine vinegar
pinch of cayenne pepper	salt and freshly ground black pepper
2 egg yolks	

METHOD

Mix the flour, mustard powder, sugar and cayenne pepper together in a saucepan. Stir in the milk, egg yolks, butter and vinegar until evenly mixed then heat very gently, whisking constantly, until thickened and smooth.

Season to taste and leave to cool, stirring occasionally to prevent a skin forming.

ABOVE *Caesar Salad Dressing*

Remoulade Sauce

MAKES ABOUT 450 ML / 15 FL OZ

This robustly-flavoured recipe is for the classic remoulade sauce, which really adds life to cold meats, eggs, fish and boiled vegetables, turning them into appetizing salads. As an alternative you could mix in celeriac, mustard and lemon juice to make celeriac remoulade.

INGREDIENTS

350 ml/12 fl oz mayonnaise, bottled or homemade (see page 19)

2 tsp *Dijon* mustard

3 tbsp pickled gherkins, chopped

3 tbsp capers, chopped

3 tbsp parsley, chopped

1 tbsp tarragon, chopped

4 anchovy fillets, chopped

METHOD

Put the mayonnaise into a bowl. Stir in the remaining ingredients.

Blue Cheese Dressing

MAKES ABOUT 350 ML / 12 FL OZ

Some people include a proportion of mayonnaise in this favourite American "classic" salad dressing, but this is the version I prefer because it is lighter, yet has a creamy taste and texture. The better the blue cheese the better the dressing; Roquefort is a traditional cheese to use and I also find Stilton and Gorgonzola make a good dressing, but Danish Blue is too harsh. Blue cheese dressing is used on and with many foods, from salad leaves to jacket potatoes.

INGREDIENTS

75 g/3 oz blue cheese, crumbled

1 garlic clove, finely crushed (optional)

225 ml/8 fl oz soured cream or Greek yogurt

about 1 tbsp white wine vinegar

about 2 tbsp parsley, chopped, or 1 tbsp chives, chopped (optional)

freshly ground black pepper

METHOD

Mash the cheese and garlic, if used, with a fork. Mix in the soured cream or yoghurt, the vinegar and parsley or chives, if using. Season with black pepper; because of the saltiness of the cheese, extra salt should not be necessary.

Cover and set aside in a cool place, but not the refrigerator if possible, for several hours. Stir before serving.

Green Goddess Dressing

MAKES ABOUT 425 ML / 15 FL OZ

A play starring the English actor George Arliss provided the name for this dressing, which was invented at the Palace Hotel in San Francisco (the hotel was destroyed in the earthquake and fire of 1906). Although it is now usual to include soured cream in the dressing, it did not feature in the original recipe. Use the dressing for fish, shellfish or vegetable salads.

INGREDIENTS

225 ml/8 fl oz Mayonnaise, bottled or homemade (see page 19)

115 ml/4 fl oz soured cream

1 garlic clove, finely chopped

3 anchovy fillets, finely chopped

4 tbsp parsley, finely chopped

4 tbsp chives, finely chopped

1 tbsp lemon juice

1 tbsp tarragon vinegar

salt and freshly ground black pepper

METHOD

Put all the ingredients into a bowl and stir together.

23

Thousand Island Dressing

MAKES ABOUT 350 ML / 12 FL OZ

The islands to which the title refers are in the St. Lawrence Seaway on the Canadian border. The original 19th-century dressing did not contain mayonnaise but was simply a vinaigrette dressing flavoured and coloured pink by paprika pepper or tomato purée, Serve with crisp green salads, egg, potato or prawn salads.

INGREDIENTS

225 ml/8 fl oz mayonnaise, bottled or homemade (see page 19)

2 tbsp stuffed olives, finely chopped

1 tbsp green pepper, finely chopped

1 tbsp onion or chives, finely chopped

1 tbsp parsley, chopped

1 hard-boiled egg, finely chopped

few drops of Tabasco sauce

salt and freshly ground black pepper

METHOD

Put the mayonnaise into a bowl. Stir in the remaining ingredients.

Sauce Vierge
(Tomato and Olive Oil Dressing)

MAKES ABOUT 350 ML / 12 FL OZ

For this dressing you really should have well-flavoured, sun-ripened tomatoes and good quality olive oil. When the sauce is left to infuse for 30 minutes there is no need for the saucepan to be over heat. The dressing goes well with all types of salads and can also be served with grilled fish or cold chicken, turkey and fish.

RIGHT *Thousand Island Dressing*

INGREDIENTS

4 well-flavoured tomatoes, peeled and deseeded

2 small garlic cloves, unpeeled

200 ml/7 fl oz virgin olive oil

2 tbsp basil or chervil, chopped

2 tbsp parsley, chopped

1 tbsp tarragon or thyme, chopped

8 coriander seeds, roasted and crushed (see page 12)

salt and freshly ground black pepper

METHOD

Cut the tomatoes into 5 mm/¼ inch dice and put into a bowl. Stir in the remaining ingredients.

Put the bowl over a saucepan of hot water, cover and leave for 30 minutes. Remove from the pan and leave until cold.

Coleslaw Dressing

MAKES ABOUT 325 ML / 11 FL OZ

Caraway seeds, a classic complement to cabbage, give this creamy dressing for the ever-popular raw cabbage salad, an extra touch of distinction.

INGREDIENTS

115 ml/4 fl oz soured cream	1 tsp mustard powder
115 ml/4 fl oz mayonnaise, bottled or homemade (see page 19)	2 tsp caraway seeds
	pinch of caster sugar
75 ml/3 fl oz cider vinegar	salt and freshly ground black pepper

METHOD

Put the soured cream, mayonnaise, vinegar, mustard powder and caraway seeds in a bowl. Whisk together until evenly combined. Add sugar and seasoning to taste.

Salad Cream

MAKES ABOUT 250 ML / 9 FL OZ

This is a traditional English creamy, cooked salad dressing. It is served with potato or any other vegetable salads, egg salads, or with fish or cold chicken. Only the yolks are used, after hard-boiling the whole eggs; the whites can be chopped and used in salads or sandwiches.

The dressing should be made about 2–2½ hours in advance as it needs time in the refrigerator to thicken to the consistency of thickish cream.

INGREDIENTS

3 eggs	4 tsp white wine vinegar
1 tbsp water	cayenne pepper
150 ml/5 fl oz double cream	salt

METHOD

Put the eggs into a saucepan and cover with cold water. Bring to the boil then boil for 9 minutes. Drain the eggs and rinse under cold running water.

Peel the eggs and remove the whites. Put the egg yolks and water into a bowl and pound together with a wooden spoon to make a smooth paste. Slowly add the cream, stirring well after each addition. Stir in the vinegar and add cayenne pepper and salt to taste. Cover and refrigerate for 2–2½ hours, after which time it will have thickened.

Sauce Louise

MAKES ABOUT 400 ML / 14 FL OZ

This zesty sauce is particularly associated with stuffed artichokes, prawns and crab.

INGREDIENTS

225 ml/8 fl oz mayonnaise, bottled or homemade (see page 19)	4 tbsp spring onions, chopped
50 ml/2 fl oz double cream	4 tbsp green pepper, chopped
2 tbsp lemon juice	few drops of Tabasco sauce
1 tsp Worcestershire sauce	

METHOD

Put the mayonnaise into a bowl. Stir in the cream and lemon juice, then the remaining ingredients.

ABOVE *Russian Dressing*

Russian Dressing

MAKES ABOUT 450 ML / 15 FL OZ

The original Russian dressing recipe contained caviar, hence the name. Serve it with green salads, vegetables, eggs, shellfish or cold meats.

INGREDIENTS

350 ml/12 fl oz mayonnaise, bottled or homemade (see page 19)

4 tbsp tomato ketchup

4 tbsp pickled gherkins, chopped

1 shallot, finely chopped

1 tsp fresh horseradish, grated

few drops of Tabasco sauce

METHOD

Put the mayonnaise into a bowl. Stir in the remaining ingredients.

Sauce Gribiche

MAKES ABOUT 375 ML / 13 FL OZ

This sauce is made like mayonnaise and although it is now often made using raw egg yolks, originally, as in this recipe, cooked ones were used. Stir into boiled vegetables to turn them into delicious salads, spoon over halved hard-boiled eggs or serve with cold meats, poultry or fish that are served with a simple green salad.

INGREDIENTS

2 hard-boiled eggs

2–3 tsp *Dijon* mustard

300 ml/½ pt sunflower or mild olive oil

2 tbsp white wine vinegar

1 tbsp capers, chopped if large

1 tbsp tarragon, chopped

1 tbsp parsley, chopped

1 tbsp chives, chopped

1 tbsp gherkins, chopped (optional)

finely grated rind of ½ lemon

salt and freshly ground black pepper

METHOD

Separate the egg whites from the yolks; reserve the whites for garnishing. Sieve the yolks and stir in the mustard.

Add the oil to the egg yolks, drop by drop, beating constantly as when making mayonnaise. After half of the oil has been incorporated, the rest can be added slightly more quickly. Stir in the remaining ingredients.

Aioli

MAKES ABOUT 375 ML / 13 FL OZ

Aioli is a type of mayonnaise which has puréed garlic cloves as a base. It comes from Provence, where it is also sometimes known as "beurre de Provence". An imitation Aioli can be made using bottled or homemade mayonnaise (see page 19) by crushing the garlic and salt as below then gradually stirring in the prepared mayonnaise.

INGREDIENTS

6–12 garlic cloves	about 300 ml/½ pt olive oil
salt and freshly ground black pepper	1½ tbsp lemon juice or white wine vinegar, or a combination of the two
2 egg yolks (see page 8)	
½–1 tsp *Dijon* mustard (optional)	

METHOD

Put the garlic and a pinch of salt into a mortar or bowl and crush them together until reduced to a paste. Work in the egg yolks, and mustard if using.

Add the oil, a few drops at a time, while stirring slowly, evenly and constantly. After half of the oil has been incorporated, add half of the lemon juice or vinegar. The rest of the oil can now be added a little more quickly but the sauce must be stirred in the same way.

Add the remaining lemon juice or vinegar and season.

Tuna Mayonnaise

MAKES ABOUT 350 ML / 12 FL OZ

Tuna mayonnaise is the classic sauce to spoon over the Italian dish of poached veal, Vitello Tonnato, *but it is so delicious that it has many other uses. For example, it perks up potato, tomato, red pepper, courgette, plain, crisp green, fish and shellfish salads and goes a treat with hard-boiled eggs and avocados. For extra zest and depth of flavour, add some chopped capers and anchovy fillets; tarragon vinegar can be used instead of lemon juice.*

INGREDIENTS

1 small garlic clove	1½ tsp *Dijon* mustard
100 g/3½ oz canned tuna, drained	225 ml/8 fl oz olive oil
about 2 tbsp lemon juice	115 ml/4 fl oz sunflower oil
leaves from a sprig of parsley	salt and freshly ground black pepper
1 egg or 2 egg yolks	

METHOD

Put the garlic, tuna, lemon juice, parsley, egg and mustard into a blender. Mix together briefly to make a smooth paste. With the motor running, slowly pour in the olive oil then the sunflower oil until well emulsified and thick.

Season to taste and add more lemon juice if liked.

2

SALAD DRESSINGS
WITH HERBS

A couple of tablespoons or so of fragrant fresh herbs are all that is needed to add vibrancy to simple salad dressings, giving them new life so that they immediately add an extra air of quality to a salad.

The type of herb you use can change the character of a salad; oregano, for example, can impart a sunny southern Italian flavour, whereas if you use mint a salad will have a clean, clear taste.

Herbs tend to darken after a little while in a salad dressing, so it is best not to add them until shortly before you are going to use the dressing.

Mint and Tomato Vinaigrette

MAKES ABOUT 225 ML /8 FL OZ

Quickly make a warm pasta salad with this chunky dressing, or use it to make an interesting salad out of cooked chicken or turkey. It is also good over salad leaves, with avocado or courgette salads, or served with warm fish such as tuna, salmon, red mullet or, more humbly, fresh mackerel.

INGREDIENTS

100 ml/3½ fl oz olive oil	3 well-flavoured tomatoes
1 tsp white wine vinegar	1 tbsp mint, chopped
1½ tsp lime juice	salt and freshly ground black pepper
1 garlic clove, finely chopped	
1 shallot, finely chopped	

METHOD

Put all the ingredients except the tomatoes and mint, into a bowl and whisk together until well emulsified.

Peel, deseed and chop the tomatoes. Stir the tomatoes and mint into the dressing and season to taste.

Herb Vinaigrette

MAKES ABOUT 115 ML /4 FL OZ

Either a single herb or a combination of herbs can be used, but try to choose ones that are complementary to the salad ingredients. If you are making the dressing in advance, do not include the herbs until shortly before it is to be served otherwise they may darken. A well-flavoured herb vinaigrette can happily be included as part of any salad.

INGREDIENTS

2 tbsp white wine vinegar or lemon juice	1 tsp *Dijon* mustard (optional)
salt and freshly ground black pepper	6 tbsp olive oil
	2 tbsp herbs, chopped

METHOD

Put the vinegar or lemon juice, seasoning and mustard, if used, into a bowl. Slowly pour in the oil in a thin steady stream, whisking until the vinaigrette has emulsified and thickened. Taste for seasoning and the level of herbs and adjust if necessary.

Special Parsley and Lemon Dressing

MAKES ABOUT 175 ML / 6 FL OZ

If possible, make the dressing a few hours or even a day ahead and leave it in a cool place, preferably not the refrigerator. Mix again before using in salads with crisp lettuce leaves, such as cos, and croutons.

INGREDIENTS

150 ml/¼ pt virgin olive oil

2 tbsp lemon juice

1 tsp grated lemon zest

2 garlic cloves, finely chopped

2 tsp parsley, chopped

1 tsp sherry vinegar

1½ tbsp Parmesan cheese, freshly grated

salt and freshly ground black pepper

METHOD

Mix all the ingredients together until well emulsified.

Oregano and Anchovy Dressing

MAKES ABOUT 200 ML / 7 FL OZ

I suggest using this dressing for grilled aubergines, peppers, courgettes and onions, with tomato or green salads, or with grilled fish. A small blender can also be used to make the dressing: put the soaked anchovy fillets, garlic, herbs and half the lemon juice into the blender or food processor and mix briefly. With the motor running, very slowly trickle in the oil until the dressing is well emulsified. Switch off the machine and add the sun-dried tomatoes and black pepper.

INGREDIENTS

75 g/3 oz canned anchovy fillets	75 ml/3 fl oz virgin olive oil
1 small garlic clove, crushed	1 tsp sun-dried tomatoes in oil, finely chopped
1½ tbsp oregano, finely chopped	freshly ground black pepper
juice of 1 lemon	

METHOD

Soak the anchovy fillets in milk for 5 minutes, then drain.

Put the anchovy fillets into a mortar with the garlic and herbs and crush together with a pestle to make a smooth paste, slowly working in half of the lemon juice.

Beat in the oil a drop at a time until half has been added. Stir in the remaining lemon juice then slowly trickle in the remaining oil, beating constantly. Lightly stir in the chopped sun-dried tomatoes and season with black pepper.

Pesto Vinaigrette

MAKES ABOUT 250 ML / 9 FL OZ

The addition of pesto sauce quickly makes an interestingly-flavoured dressing that is also versatile; it goes with green, pasta and nearly all vegetable salads (beetroot is one exception I've found), and with egg, shellfish, chicken, turkey and beef salads.

INGREDIENTS

5–6 tbsp white wine vinegar	150 ml/¼ pt olive oil
4 tsp pesto sauce	salt and freshly ground black pepper

METHOD

Put 5 tablespoons of the vinegar and the pesto sauce into a bowl. Slowly pour in the oil, whisking until emulsified.

Season to taste and add more vinegar if liked.

RIGHT *Oregano and Anchovy Dressing*

Tarragon and Sesame Dressing

MAKES ABOUT 100 ML / 3½ FL OZ

With its nutty taste, this dressing complements sliced, well-flavoured ripe tomatoes. In place of the sesame oil you could use walnut oil.

INGREDIENTS

4 tsp tarragon, chopped

1 tbsp *Dijon* mustard

2 tbsp lemon juice

2 tbsp sesame oil

pinch of sugar (optional)

salt and freshly ground black pepper

METHOD

Put all the ingredients into a bowl and whisk together.

Parsley Dressing

MAKES ABOUT 225 ML / 8 FL OZ

The flavour of parsley does not vary much from season to season, so this is a useful, and welcome, herb dressing for the winter, especially as it happily combines with winter vegetable salads. To make the dressing in a small blender or food processor, put the garlic, fennel seeds and a pinch of salt into the machine, mix briefly then, with the motor running, slowly pour in the oil, adding 2 tablespoons of the parsley towards the end. Pour into a bowl and stir in the remaining parsley, the spring onions, tarragon and black pepper.

INGREDIENTS

2 garlic cloves

¼ tsp fennel seeds

salt and freshly ground black pepper

leaves from a large bunch of parsley

about 2 tbsp white or red wine vinegar

rind of 1 lime, finely grated

175 ml/6 fl oz olive oil

3 spring onions, finely chopped

1 tsp tarragon, chopped (optional)

METHOD

Put the garlic, fennel seeds and a pinch of salt into a mortar or bowl. Crush together with a pestle or the end of a rolling-pin until reduced to a paste, adding 2 tablespoons of the parsley towards the end.

Stir in the vinegar and lime rind. Slowly trickle in the oil, whisking until well emulsified.

Stir in the remaining parsley, the spring onions and tarragon and season with black pepper.

Tomato and Basil Dressing

MAKES ABOUT 300 ML / ½ PT

A light, clean-tasting dressing for fish and shellfish, pasta, egg, chicken or avocado salads. The walnut oil enhances the flavour of the tomatoes and if you are able to use well-flavoured, sun-ripened tomatoes they should be sweet enough for the dressing. If not, add a little sugar.

INGREDIENTS

1 tbsp olive oil

2 tbsp walnut oil

2 tbsp white wine vinegar

1 tbsp sherry vinegar

3 well-flavoured tomatoes

18–20 basil leaves, chopped

pinch of caster sugar (optional)

salt and freshly ground black pepper

METHOD

Pour the oils and vinegars into a bowl. Whisk together.

Peel, deseed and finely chop the tomatoes then stir into the dressing with the basil. Add a little caster sugar if necessary, then season to taste.

39

ABOVE *Chive and Lemon Vinaigrette*

Chive and Lemon Vinaigrette

MAKES ABOUT 175 ML / 6 FL OZ

Use this dressing to make a delicious, light potato salad by tossing it with warm potatoes, particularly new ones, and finely chopped spring onions, then leaving until cold.

INGREDIENTS	
1 garlic clove	1½ tsp wholegrain mustard
salt and freshly ground black pepper	4 tbsp virgin olive oil
4 tbsp lemon juice	2 tbsp chives, chopped
rind of 1 lemon, finely grated	

METHOD

Put the garlic and a pinch of salt into a bowl. Crush together, then stir in the lemon rind and juice and the mustard until smooth.

Slowly pour in the oil, whisking constantly, until well emulsified.

Add the chives and season with black pepper.

Herb, Lemon and Caper Dressing

MAKES ABOUT 300 ML / ½ PT

This dressing goes well with shellfish, green, cucumber, courgette or egg salads, or with grilled fish, especially salmon or firm fish such as monkfish or fresh cod, and fish cakes.

INGREDIENTS	
½ garlic clove	4 tbsp capers
salt and freshly ground black pepper	2 tbsp chives, chopped
4 tbsp lemon juice	2 tbsp dill, chopped
	150 ml/¼ pt olive oil

METHOD

Put the garlic and a pinch of salt into a mortar. Crush together with a pestle until reduced to a paste.

Stir in the lemon juice, capers and herbs. Slowly trickle in the oil, whisking until well emulsified. Season with black pepper.

Herb, Garlic and Mustard Dressing

MAKES ABOUT 250 ML / 9 FL OZ

This is a quite strongly flavoured dressing so is best used for more robust salads such as salade Nicoise.

INGREDIENTS

1–2 garlic cloves	1 tsp *Dijon* mustard
salt and freshly ground black pepper	50 ml/2 fl oz red wine vinegar
leaves from 4–5 sprigs of thyme	175 ml/6 fl oz olive oil
leaves and fine stems from a small bunch of chervil	

METHOD

Put the garlic, herbs and a pinch of salt into a bowl. Crush together then stir in the vinegar and the mustard until smooth.

Slowly pour in the oil, whisking constantly, until well emulsified. Season with black pepper.

Basil Dressing

MAKES ABOUT 175 ML / 6 FL OZ

I love basil but as it is always at its best when it has basked in glorious sunshine, I reserve making this dressing until the summer. Then I use it for many salads, such as warm pasta, shellfish, green, potato, courgette, egg, cheese and grilled vegetables.

INGREDIENTS

2 garlic cloves	1 tbsp white wine vinegar
leaves from 1 large bunch of basil	6 tbsp virgin olive oil
salt and freshly ground black pepper	2 tbsp freshly grated Parmesan cheese

METHOD

Put the garlic, basil leaves, dash of salt and vinegar into a small blender. Mix briefly then, with the motor running, slowly pour in the oil until well emulsified.

Transfer to a bowl. Stir in the cheese and season with black pepper.

Coriander, Caper and Lime Dressing

MAKES ABOUT 225 ML / 8 FL OZ

Try tossing this piquant dressing with warm potatoes or celeriac then leaving to cool, or use for seafood salads, or spoon over fried foods such as fish or sliced cheeses such as haloumi or feta.

INGREDIENTS

1 garlic clove, finely chopped	4 tbsp virgin olive oil
1½ tsp wholegrain mustard	3–4 tbsp capers
finely grated rind and juice of 2 limes	3 tbsp coriander, chopped
1 tbsp white wine vinegar	freshly ground black pepper

METHOD

Put the garlic, mustard, lime rind and juice and vinegar into a bowl and mix together. Slowly pour in the oil, whisking constantly, until well emulsified. Stir in the capers and coriander. Season with black pepper.

3

SALAD DRESSINGS
WITH SPICES

Aromatic spices from around the world add their magical touch to salad dressings. These then quickly turn simple salad ingredients into exotic treats. The salads do not have to be authentically ethnic but can be made of any ingredients you like.

Black Bean, Ginger and Watercress Dressing

MAKES ABOUT 150 ML / 5 FL OZ

If you do not have any rice wine, you can use 1 tablespoon rice vinegar and 1 tablespoon water instead. Serve with fish salads made of salmon or firm white fish such as monkfish, chicken, young spinach leaves, warm Chinese egg thread or cellophane noodles.

INGREDIENTS

1 tbsp salted black beans, coarsely chopped	2 tsp grated fresh ginger
	2 tbsp rice wine
1 tbsp groundnut or grapeseed oil	40 g/1½ oz fine stems and leaves of watercress
2 tsp sesame oil	freshly ground black pepper

METHOD

Steep the black beans in 1–2 tablespoons of hot water for 15 minutes. Drain and dry on paper towels.

Put the black beans, oils, ginger and rice wine into a bowl and whisk together until emulsified. Stir in the watercress and season with black pepper.

Chilli and Ginger Dressing

MAKES 175 ML / 6 FL OZ

Use this zesty dressing to dress pork, beef, chicken, duck or fish salads.

INGREDIENTS

175 ml/6 fl oz grapeseed oil	2.5 cm/1 in piece fresh ginger, grated
2 tbsp white wine vinegar	2 spring onions, finely chopped
1–2 fresh green chillies, deseeded and finely chopped	salt and freshly ground black pepper

METHOD

Whisk together the oil and vinegar until emulsified.

Add the chilli, ginger and spring onion. Mix together then season to taste.

Nutty Coriander Dressing

MAKES ABOUT 400 ML / 14 FL OZ

As this is a dark sauce it is appropriate for serving over dark leaves such as radicchio and oak leaves. It also marries well with warm Oriental noodle salads or stir-fried vegetable salads.

INGREDIENTS

75 ml/3 fl oz peanut oil

2 tbsp sesame oil

5 tbsp coriander, chopped

4 tbsp light soy sauce

4 tbsp red wine vinegar

3 tbsp crunchy peanut butter

3 tbsp black bean sauce

50 g/2 oz fresh ginger, grated

2 tsp chilli sauce

1 tbsp caster sugar

METHOD

Put all the ingredients into a food processor and mix until smooth. Alternatively, beat together in a bowl.

Chilli and Coriander Vinaigrette

MAKES ABOUT 225 ML / 8 FL OZ

Containing chillies, ground cumin and fresh coriander this dressing is an obvious candidate for using over Mexican-style bean and corn salads.

INGREDIENTS

3 fresh green chillies, deseeded and finely chopped

½ tsp ground cumin

40 ml/1½ oz cider vinegar

salt

115 ml/4 fl oz peanut oil

leaves from a small bunch of coriander, chopped

METHOD

Put the chillies, cumin, vinegar and salt into a bowl. Whisk together. Slowly pour in the oil, whisking constantly, until the dressing is well emulsified. Stir in the coriander just before serving.

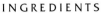

Coconut and Peanut Dressing

MAKES ABOUT 175 ML / 6 FL OZ

To roast the Szechuan peppercorns, see page 51, then grind them in a spice grinder or crush them very finely in a pestle and mortar. Serve over Chinese noodle salads or raw vegetable salads.

INGREDIENTS

1½ tbsp groundnut oil

2 garlic cloves, crushed

50 g/2 oz coconut cream block, chopped

4 tsp soy sauce

2 tbsp rice vinegar

3 tbsp peanut butter

good pinch soft dark brown sugar

large pinch of ground roasted Szechuan peppercorns

freshly ground black pepper

METHOD

Heat the oil into a small heavy frying pan, add the garlic and fry gently for 1–2 minutes. Add the coconut cream and stir until melted. Stir in the remaining ingredients until well mixed.

Ginger and Coriander Vinaigrette

MAKES ABOUT 225 ML / 8 FL OZ

The coriander is added at the last minute otherwise it will darken. A garnish of toasted sesame seeds complements the dressing. Toss with salad leaves such as curly endive, cos, batavia, watercress or young spinach, use for cheese salads, or to dress fish such as sea bass, tuna or salmon, or for chicken or pork.

INGREDIENTS

1.25 cm/½ in piece of ginger, grated

1 shallot, finely chopped

juice of 1 lime

1 tbsp soy sauce

2 tbsp rice wine vinegar

115 ml/4 fl oz olive oil

1 tbsp dark sesame oil

salt and freshly ground black pepper

½ bunch of coriander, coarsely chopped

METHOD

Put the ginger, shallots, lime juice, soy sauce and vinegar into a bowl and whisk together.

Trickle in the olive oil, whisking vigorously, then whisk in the sesame oil. Season to taste. Add the coriander just before serving.

Indonesian Peanut Dressing

MAKES ABOUT 425 ML / 15 FL OZ

This dressing is an essential part of the Indonesian mixed vegetable, tofu and flat omelette salad, gado gado, *although it is served separately rather than over the salad ingredients. It can also be served as a dressing for warm potato, French bean, cauliflower, courgette or celery salads. If the dressing is prepared in advance, it may separate: this can be rectified by heating gently and stirring in about 1 tablespoon of water.*

INGREDIENTS

2 tbsp groundnut oil	175 ml/6 fl oz coconut milk
1 onion, finely chopped	1½ tsp soy sauce
1 garlic clove, finely crushed	juice of ½ lime
pinch of crushed red chillies	1 tsp brown sugar
115 g/4 oz unsalted roasted peanuts	salt and freshly ground black pepper

METHOD

Heat the oil in a frying pan, and fry the onion until lightly browned. Add the garlic and chillies and fry until the onion is golden.

Meanwhile, put the peanuts into a food processor and grind to a coarse paste. Stir in the coconut milk, soy sauce, lime juice, sugar and nut paste, mixing well until smooth and creamy.

Szechuan Peppercorn Dressing

MAKES ABOUT 400 ML / 14 FL OZ

This dressing, which has quite a pronounced flavour, will lose its colour, though not its flavour, if kept for more than a few hours. Serve it over duck, chicken and cold pasta salads.

INGREDIENTS

1 tbsp Szechuan peppercorns	1 tbsp parsley
3 garlic cloves	1 tbsp dill
juice of 6 limes	1 tbsp sugar
1 tbsp coriander	salt and freshly ground black pepper

RIGHT *Indonesian Peanut Dressing*

METHOD

Put the peppercorns into a dry small, heavy frying pan and heat until fragrant. Tip into a blender and add the remaining ingredients. Mix until smooth.

Curry Dressing

MAKES ABOUT 150 ML / 5 FL OZ

I use a medium curry paste; if you use a hot or mild one do not forget to adjust the amount to add to the dressing accordingly. The dressing gives character to salads containing fruit, or salads with watercress or spinach, or served over prawns.

INGREDIENTS

1 tsp curry paste	1½ tbsp white vinegar or lemon juice
1 garlic clove	6 tbsp grapeseed oil
salt and freshly ground black pepper	about ½ tsp grated fresh ginger (optional)

METHOD

Put the curry paste, garlic and a pinch of salt into a mortar or small bowl and crush together to a paste using a pestle or the end of a rolling pin.

Whisk in the vinegar, then slowly pour in the oil, whisking constantly until well emulsified.

Add the ginger, if liked, and season to taste with black pepper.

Sesame Dressing

MAKES 225 ML / 8 FL OZ

I use this dressing over Asian noodle salads that are served hot. Chinese egg noodles can be cooked in advance, cooled then kept covered in the refrigerator. Just before serving, reheat the noodles in a covered colander over a saucepan of boiling water for 5–7 minutes.

INGREDIENTS

3 tbsp peanut oil	½–1 fresh red chilli, deseeded and finely chopped
2 tbsp sesame oil	
4 tbsp soy sauce	
1 garlic clove, crushed	4 tbsp chopped coriander
3 tbsp toasted sesame seeds	

METHOD

Mix together all the ingredients except the coriander. Immediately before serving, add the coriander leaves.

Satay Dressing

MAKES ABOUT 500 ML / 18 FL OZ

If you cannot buy roasted unsalted peanuts, toast unsalted peanuts under the grill until browned, stirring frequently so they brown evenly.

Serve the dressing over pork, beef, chicken or shellfish satays, or kebabs and garnish with lime wedges.

INGREDIENTS

75 g/3 oz roasted unsalted peanuts	2 tbsp soft dark brown sugar
1 garlic clove	squeeze of lime juice
2 tbsp red curry paste	pinch of hot chilli powder
400 ml/14 fl oz coconut milk	

METHOD

Put the peanuts, garlic, curry paste and a little of the coconut milk into a blender and mix to a paste. Add the remaining coconut milk and sugar. Mix until smooth.

Pour the ingredients into a saucepan and add the lemon juice. Boil for 2 minutes then simmer gently for 10 minutes, stirring occasionally to prevent sticking. Add a little water if the sauce becomes too thick. Add chilli powder to taste. Serve warm.

4

SALAD DRESSINGS
WITH FRUITS AND NUTS

Fruits can be used in salad dressings in place of all
or part of the vinegar and have the additional
bonus of giving the dressing more flavour and
character. Each fruit has its own special taste so if you
make basically the same dressing with different fruits
you will get quite different results.

Nuts contribute both flavour and texture to salad
dressings. To maximize the flavour of nuts, spread
them on a baking sheet and toast in a preheated oven
at 180°C/350°F/Gas mark 4 for 15–20 minutes, stirring
the nuts occasionally, until they are brown and crisp.
Buy nuts in small quantities and store them in a cool,
dark place. Before using any nuts, make sure that they
are absolutely fresh without any hint of rancidity.

Mango Vinaigrette

MAKES ABOUT 300 ML / ½ PT

Use this dressing to accompany smoked chicken, turkey or pork.

INGREDIENTS

1 ripe mango, peeled and sliced	1 tbsp white wine vinegar
1 small to medium fresh red chilli, deseeded and chopped	115 ml/4 fl oz olive oil
	salt and freshly ground black pepper

METHOD

Put all the ingredients into a blender and mix until smooth.

Orange Vinaigrette

MAKES ABOUT 200 ML / 7 FL OZ

Use this dressing to finish a refreshing salad of thinly sliced fennel and oranges, or a grated carrot salad. With a pinch of caraway seeds added it can be used for beetroot salads.

INGREDIENTS

4 tbsp orange juice	1 tsp balsamic vinegar
1 tsp finely grated orange rind	1 shallot, finely chopped
1 tbsp white wine vinegar	6 tbsp virgin olive oil
	salt and freshly ground black pepper

METHOD

Put all the orange juice and rind, the vinegars and shallot into a bowl. Slowly pour in the oil, whisking until well emulsified. Season to taste.

Lemon Vinaigrette

MAKES ABOUT 175 ML / 6 FL OZ

Lemon rind and juice give this dressing a good lemony flavour. It is especially good for fennel or chicory salads.

INGREDIENTS

1 garlic clove	juice of 1 large lemon
salt and freshly ground black pepper	¼ tsp paprika pepper
finely grated rind of ⅓ large lemon	pinch of cayenne pepper
	6 tbsp virgin olive oil

METHOD

Put the garlic and a pinch of salt into a mortar or bowl and crush together with a pestle or the end of a rolling pin until reduced to a paste.

Stir in the lemon rind and juice, the paprika and cayenne pepper. Slowly pour in the oil, whisking until well emulsified.

Roast Tomato and Garlic Vinaigrette

MAKES ABOUT 225 ML / 6 FL OZ

Pour the dressing over grilled red peppers, courgettes, aubergines and onions, or toss with pasta.

INGREDIENTS

1 large ridged tomato

3 plump garlic cloves, unpeeled

1 tsp sherry vinegar

4 tbsp virgin olive oil

salt and freshly ground black pepper

METHOD

Preheat the grill. Grill the tomato and garlic until softened, charred and blistered. Leave to cool then peel them. Deseed and chop the tomato.

Put the garlic and tomato into a blender and mix until smooth. Add the vinegar then, with the motor running, slowly pour in the oil until well emulsified.

Poppy Seed Vinaigrette

MAKES ABOUT 250 ML / 9 FL OZ

The light nutty crunch of the poppy seeds adds a fillip to avocado salads, green salads of leaves such as curly endive, and savoury fruit salads.

INGREDIENTS

½ tsp English mustard powder

¼ tsp ground ginger

½ red onion, grated

3 tbsp red wine vinegar

1 tbsp clear honey

1 tbsp poppy seeds

150 ml/5 fl oz peanut oil

salt and freshly ground black pepper

METHOD

Put the mustard powder, ground ginger, onion, vinegar, honey and poppy seeds into a bowl. Whisk together.

Slowly pour in the oil, whisking constantly, until the dressing is well emulsified. Season to taste.

RIGHT *Roast Tomato and Garlic Vinaigrette*

Orange and Lemon Dressing

MAKES ABOUT 250 ML / 9 FL OZ

Carrot and beetroot salads marry well with this quite complex flavoured dressing, as do salads that contain fruit.

INGREDIENTS

finely grated rind and juice of 1 orange

4 tsp lemon juice

¼ tsp fennel seeds, crushed

1 tsp balsamic vinegar

3 spring onions, white parts only, finely chopped

salt and freshly ground black pepper

5 tbsp olive oil

1 tbsp hazelnut oil

3 tbsp mixed chopped herbs such as chervil, parsley and chives

METHOD

Put the orange rind and juice, the lemon juice, fennel seeds, vinegar, spring onions and salt into a bowl and mix together. Slowly pour in the oils, whisking until well emulsified. Add the herbs and season with black pepper.

Creamy Orange and Hazelnut Dressing

MAKES ABOUT 175 ML / 6 FL OZ

This dressing works a treat over a salad of grilled salmon with lamb's lettuce, spinach, watercress, or it can just be served over the salad leaves without the salmon. It also complements beetroot, carrot, fennel and chicory salads.

INGREDIENTS

3 tbsp orange juice

2 tbsp sherry vinegar

2 tbsp double cream

1 tbsp orange liqueur (optional)

100 ml/3½ fl oz hazelnut oil

50 g/2 oz hazelnuts, toasted and chopped

salt and freshly ground pepper

METHOD

Put the orange juice, vinegar, double cream and liqueur into a bowl. Mix together. Slowly pour in the oil, whisking, until the dressing emulsifies.

Add the hazelnuts and season to taste.

Walnut Dressing

MAKES ABOUT 115 ML / 4 FL OZ

LLYFRGELL / LIBRARY
COLEG MENAI
LLANGEFNI
YNYS MÔN
LL77 7HY
Tel: (01248)

Balsamic vinegar adds richness to the dressing; the amount you will need to add will depend on the richness of the vinegar and how richly flavoured you want the dressing to be. For a lighter taste use some white wine vinegar in conjunction with the balsamic vinegar. Walnut dressing has a particular affinity with cheese, watercress and spinach salads, and also harmonizes with cabbage and firm salad leaves.

INGREDIENTS

25 g/1 oz walnut halves	2 tbsp balsamic vinegar
3 tbsp olive oil	salt and freshly ground black pepper
3 tbsp walnut oil	

METHOD

Preheat an oven to 180°C/350°F/Gas mark 4. Spread the nuts on a baking tray and put in the oven for about 15 minutes until crisp and browned. Chop the nuts. Put the oils and vinegar into a bowl. Whisk until well blended.

Add the nuts and season to taste.

Mediterranean Dressing

MAKES ABOUT 250 ML / 9 FL OZ

Bursting with the heat-soaked flavours that result from basking in the Mediterranean sunshine, this dressing is ideal for a salad made of cubed firm white bread (flavoured with herbs or garlic if liked) and crisp salad leaves. It is also good spooned over grilled cheese such as haloumi, or tossed with pasta.

INGREDIENTS

2 oil-soaked sun-dried tomatoes

1 small garlic clove

1 tbsp capers

about 8 pitted black olives

1½ tbsp red or white wine vinegar

7 tbsp virgin olive oil

pinch of sugar (optional)

freshly ground black pepper

METHOD

Finely chop the tomatoes, garlic, capers and olives.

Put into a bowl and add the vinegar. Slowly pour in the oil, whisking constantly, until well emulsified. Season with black pepper.

Rich Sun-dried Tomato Dressing

MAKES ABOUT 250 ML / 9 FL OZ

Warm pasta salads benefit from tossing in this richly flavoured dressing. It also adds life to potato salads and barbecued sweetcorn.

INGREDIENTS

4 oil-soaked sun-dried tomatoes

1 plump garlic clove

about 2 tsp wholegrain mustard

4 tbsp red wine vinegar

2 tbsp sun-dried tomato paste

4 tbsp oil from the jar of sun-dried tomatoes

5 tbsp extra virgin olive oil

salt and freshly ground black pepper

METHOD

Put the sun-dried tomatoes, garlic, mustard, vinegar and paste into a blender. With the motor running, slowly pour in the sun-dried tomato oil and the olive oil and mix briefly. Season to taste and add more mustard, if liked.

ABOVE *Mediterranean Dressing*

Lemon and Lime Cream Dressing

MAKES ABOUT 350 ML / 12 FL OZ

Lighter than mayonnaise (and without egg yolks) this clean-tasting dressing can be used as an alternative to mayonnaise to dress prawn, scallop and lobster salads, or chicken or turkey salads.

INGREDIENTS

finely grated rind and juice of 1 large lime

finely grated rind and juice of ½ lemon

4 plump spring onions, finely chopped

salt and freshly ground black pepper

2 tsp caster sugar

5 tbsp olive oil

150 ml/¼ pt double cream

few drops of Tabasco sauce

METHOD

Put the lemon and lime rinds and juices, the spring onions, salt and sugar into a bowl. Slowly trickle in the oil, whisking until well emulsified.

Gradually whisk in the cream. Add Tabasco sauce and black pepper to taste.

Sweet and Savoury Dressing

MAKES ABOUT 250 ML / 9 FL OZ

Use this dressing for fruit salads served as a first course, such as mixed melons. Chopped mint, grated fresh ginger or a sprinkling of ground cinnamon are good finishing touches.

INGREDIENTS

2 tbsp clear honey

75 ml/3 fl oz port

juice of 3 lemons

salt and freshly ground black pepper

METHOD

Put the honey, port and lemon into a bowl. Stir together then season to taste.

Coconut and Lemon Dressing

MAKES ABOUT 200 ML / 7 FL OZ

Serve with fish or shellfish or Chinese noodle salads. Garnish the salad with basil leaves.

INGREDIENTS

1 tbsp groundnut or grapeseed oil

175 g/6 oz coconut cream block, chopped

2 tbsp rice wine

7.5 cm/3 in piece of lemon grass, crushed and thinly sliced

large pinch of five spice powder

salt and freshly ground black pepper

METHOD

Heat the oil in a small heavy frying pan. Add the coconut cream and heat gently, stirring, until it has melted. Stir in the remaining ingredients until evenly blended.

5

MAYONNAISE-BASED DRESSINGS

———

Mayonnaise is the second universally most well-known salad dressing after French dressing. Mayonnaise is most often served plain but there are so many ways in which it can easily be flavoured to make excitingly different sauces to enliven salads – I have not yet found a herb or spice that cannot be blended with mayonnaise to good effect. Even vegetables such as watercress (see page 68) can be added, or you can add flavour and colour by blending mayonnaise with puréed cooked spinach or puréed grilled red peppers.

Homemade mayonnaise is very easy to make (see page 19) but you may prefer to use bottled mayonnaise. The somewhat lifeless flavour of bottled mayonnaise can be improved by beating in a couple of tablespoons of virgin olive oil, as well as other flavourings.

Simple Flavoured Mayonnaises

ABOVE *Watercress Mayonnaise*

Watercress Mayonnaise
Remove the tough stalks from a bunch of watercress. Chop the leaves and fine stems and add to 350 ml/12 fl oz homemade mayonnaise (see page 19), or bottled mayonnaise.

Chantilly Mayonnaise
Whip 75 ml/3 fl oz whipping or double cream until it stands in soft peaks then gently fold into 350 ml/12 fl oz homemade mayonnaise (see page 19), or bottled mayonnaise.

Horseradish Mayonnaise
Add 1–2 tablespoons lemon juice and 2 tablespoons freshly grated horseradish to 350 ml/12 fl oz homemade mayonnaise (see page 19), or bottled mayonnaise.

Herb Mayonnaise
Add about 6 tablespoons chopped herbs to 350 ml/12 fl oz homemade mayonnaise (see page 19), or bottled mayonnaise.

Caper Mayonnaise
Add 4 teaspoons chopped capers and 1 teaspoon tarragon vinegar to 350 ml/12 fl oz homemade mayonnaise (see page 19), or bottled mayonnaise.

Extra Light Mayonnaise
Whisk 1–2 egg whites until they form stiff peaks then fold into 350 ml/12 fl oz homemade mayonnaise (see page 19), or bottled mayonnaise.

Light Mayonnaise
Stir together yogurt and homemade mayonnaise (see page 19) or bottled mayonnaise in the proportions you want. I particularly like to use Greek yogurt for this.

Lemon Mayonnaise
If making homemade mayonnaise (see page 19), use lemon juice rather than vinegar, and add 2 tablespoons finely grated lemon rind to the egg yolks. If using bottled mayonnaise, add the grated lemon rind to the mayonnaise.

Sauce Verte

MAKES 350 ML / 12 FL OZ

A favourite dressing for cold summer platters of fish, especially salmon, or poultry. The dressing also complements hard-boiled eggs and many cold, boiled vegetables. I use it in egg and chicken sandwiches.

INGREDIENTS

115 g/4 oz mixed herbs and leaves such as sorrel, watercress and spinach

350 ml/12 fl oz bottled homemade mayonnaise (see page 19)

METHOD

Add the herbs and leaves to a saucepan of boiling water and boil for 30 seconds. Drain and rinse under cold running water. Drain well and squeeze dry.

Chop finely or purée in a blender. Add the herbs and leaves to the mayonnaise. Cover and chill.

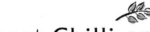

Roast Chilli and Szechuan Peppercorn Mayonnaise

MAKES 325 ML / 11 FL OZ

This dressing is not as thick as ordinary mayonnaise. It can be used to lend an oriental flavour to all manner of salads.

INGREDIENTS

115 g/4 oz fresh red chillies

2 egg yolks (see page 8)

1 plump garlic clove

salt

2 tbsp orange juice

225 ml/8 fl oz mild olive oil (or 115 ml/4 fl oz olive oil and 115 ml/4 fl oz groundnut oil)

pinch of roasted Szechuan peppercorns (see page 51)

METHOD

Preheat the grill. Grill the chillies until the skins are charred and blistered. Leave to cool then peel off the skins, slice in half and discard the seeds.

Put the chillies, egg yolks, garlic, salt and orange juice into a blender. Mix together briefly. With the motor running, slowly trickle in the oil. Add Szechuan pepper to taste.

Roast Garlic Mayonnaise

Roasting garlic softens its flavour and gives it a delicious smoky taste, which, in turn, adds an enticing flavour to the mayonnaise. If liked, 2 mashed anchovy fillets can be added with the egg yolks.

INGREDIENTS

2 garlic bulbs, unpeeled

2 sprigs of thyme or rosemary

2 tbsp olive oil

2 egg yolks
(see page 8)

2–3 tsp lemon juice

300 ml/½ pt virgin olive oil

salt and freshly ground black pepper

METHOD

Preheat the oven to 180°C/350°F/Gas mark 4. Put each garlic bulb on a piece of greaseproof paper. Add a thyme or rosemary sprig and trickle over 1 tablespoon of olive oil. Fold up the greaseproof paper to enclose the garlic and seal the edges together firmly to seal well. Put on a baking sheet and bake for 35–40 minutes until the garlic is soft.

Allow the garlic to cool slightly then squeeze the garlic cloves from their skins, into a bowl. Add the egg yolks and 1 teaspoon of the lemon juice. Beat hard.

Beat in a drop of virgin olive oil at a time until half of the oil has been added. Add another 1 teaspoon of lemon juice then slowly trickle in the remaining oil, beating hard, constantly.

Season and add more lemon juice, if necessary.

Saffron Mayonnaise

MAKES ABOUT 350 ML / 12 FL OZ

Saffron is expensive but only a few strands are needed to make this luxurious-tasting mayonnaise. It adds a real sense of occasion whenever it is used with shellfish salads, for example. To make saffron mayonnaise from bottled mayonnaise, use 1 tablespoon lemon juice and prepare the saffron in the same way. Add to bottled garlic mayonnaise.

INGREDIENTS

2 tbsp white wine vinegar	1 garlic clove
pinch of saffron strands	salt and freshly ground black pepper
2 egg yolks (see page 8)	300 ml/½ pt olive oil

METHOD

Pour the vinegar into a small saucepan. Boil for 2 minutes. Add the saffron, remove from the heat and leave to infuse for 5 minutes.

Put the egg yolks, saffron liquid, garlic and a pinch of salt into a blender. Mix together. With the motor running, slowly trickle in the oil until well emulsified. Season with black pepper.

Piquant Coriander Mayonnaise

MAKES ABOUT 300 ML / ½ PT

I like to serve this delightful dressing with jumbo prawns, crab, lobster, chicken, potato, egg or avocado salads or with grilled or fried lamb or fish and fish cakes.

INGREDIENTS

1 egg (see page 8)	4 small cornichons (continental gherkins), finely chopped
1 small garlic clove	
½ tsp English mustard powder	1½ tbsp small capers
salt and freshly ground black pepper	1 tbsp coriander, chopped
175 ml/6 fl oz mild olive oil	2 tsp lime juice

METHOD

Put the egg, garlic, mustard powder and seasoning into a blender. Mix briefly, then with the motor still running, very slowly trickle in the oil. Transfer the sauce to a bowl and stir in the remaining ingredients.

Ginger and Spring Onion Mayonnaise

MAKES ABOUT 300 ML / ½ PT

To make the ginger juice needed for this recipe, crush a piece of peeled ginger in a garlic press. Use to dress chicken, pork, fish or shellfish, and vegetable salads.

INGREDIENTS

2 egg yolks (see page 8)

salt

½–1 tsp ginger juice

115 ml/4 fl oz olive oil

115 ml/4 fl oz peanut oil

2 tbsp spring onion, chopped

freshly ground black pepper

METHOD

Put the egg yolks, salt and ½ teaspoon of ginger juice into a blender. Mix briefly. With the motor running, slowly trickle in the oils; add the spring onions almost at the end so they become finely chopped but are not reduced to a pulp.

Season with black pepper. Add more ginger juice if necessary.

Sesame Seed and Garlic Mayonnaise

MAKES ABOUT 325 ML / 11 FL OZ

Rice vinegar is used for this recipe so the dressing is mild, getting its character from the spring onions, roasted sesame seeds and a little garlic (you can increase the garlic if liked). To roast sesame seeds, put them into a dry, heavy, small frying pan and heat gently until they are light brown in colour and smell toasted.

INGREDIENTS

2 egg yolks (see page 8)

2 garlic cloves

salt

2 tsp white rice vinegar

225 ml/8 fl oz mild olive oil (or 115 ml/4 fl oz olive oil and 115 ml/ 4 fl oz peanut oil)

4 tbsp spring onions, chopped

1 tbsp sesame seeds, roasted

freshly ground black pepper

METHOD

Put the egg yolks, garlic, salt and vinegar into a blender. Mix together briefly. With the motor running, slowly trickle in the olive oil; add the spring onions almost at the end.

Transfer to a bowl. Fold in the sesame seeds and season with black pepper.

Curry Mayonnaise

MAKES ABOUT 225 ML / 8 FL OZ

Use for chicken, ham, egg or potato salads, to liven up left over roast turkey, or in chicken, ham or egg sandwiches.

INGREDIENTS

6 tbsp bottled or home-made mayonnaise (see page 19)

6 tbsp double cream

1 tbsp curry paste

1 tbsp shallot or red onion, finely chopped

juice of ½ lemon

1 tbsp mango chutney

salt and freshly ground black pepper

METHOD

LEFT *Sesame Seed and Garlic Mayonnaise*

Put all the ingredients into a bowl and stir together. Cover and leave to stand for at least 30 minutes.

6

SALAD DRESSINGS WITH YOGURT, CHEESE AND CREAM

Yogurt, cream and cheeses have a variety of tastes, consistencies and fat contents, so they can be used to add different flavours and textures to dressings. Yogurt can be used to lower the fat content, therefore calories and cholesterol of both the French dressing type and mayonnaise type. As well as adding richness to dressings, cream can also be used instead of oil; this is also less fattening than a dressing based on oil because, measure for measure, cream contains fewer calories.

Cream, curd and ricotta cheeses make richer, thicker dressings than cream, while blue cheeses add piquancy.

For people who cannot tolerate, or prefer not to eat dairy products, a tofu-based mayonnaise is included at the end of the chapter.

Yogurt Vinaigrette

MAKES ABOUT 350 ML / 12 FL OZ

This is a lighter tasting, fresher alternative to ordinary vinaigrette, and can be used in the same ways. Walnut or hazelnut oil can be substituted for half of the olive oil, depending on the salad.

INGREDIENTS

6 tbsp plain yogurt	about 2 tbsp water (optional)
2 tbsp sherry vinegar	pinch of caster sugar
4 tbsp olive oil	salt and freshly ground white or black pepper
2 tsp *Dijon* mustard	

METHOD

Put the yogurt, vinegar, oil and mustard into a bowl and mix together. If the vinaigrette is too thick (thicknesses of yogurts vary), add a little water. Add sugar and seasoning to taste.

Yogurt Salad Dressing

MAKES ABOUT 325 ML / 11 FL OZ

An easy to make, light, fresh tasting dressing that will liven up green salads. For extra interest, add 25 g/1 oz chopped herbs such as chives, or mixed herbs. The dressing will not keep very long as the yogurt acts on the cream and turns it into rich yogurt.

INGREDIENTS

150 ml/¼ pt plain yogurt	pinch of caster sugar
150 ml/¼ pt double cream	salt and freshly ground white or black pepper
juice of 1 lemon	

METHOD

Put the yogurt, cream and lemon juice into a bowl and stir together. Add sugar and seasoning to taste.

Mustard Yogurt Dressing

MAKES ABOUT 300 ML / ½ PINT

A light but well-flavoured dressing for spinach, potato or other vegetable salads.

INGREDIENTS

225 ml/8 fl oz plain yogurt

1 tbsp finely chopped spring onion

1 tbsp *Dijon* mustard

1 tbsp chopped parsley or chives

salt and pepper

METHOD

Put all the ingredients into a bowl and stir together until evenly mixed. Cover and chill before using.

Yogurt and Orange Dressing

MAKES ABOUT 300 ML / ½ PT

Use for first course fruit salads, such as melon and orange, and garnish with mint.

INGREDIENTS

3 tbsp orange juice	225 ml/8 fl oz thick plain yogurt
1 tbsp clear honey	salt and freshly ground white pepper

METHOD

Stir the orange juice into the honey. Add the orange juice mixture to the yogurt and stir together. Season to taste. Cover and chill.

Yogurt and Tahini Dressing

MAKES ABOUT 200 ML / 7 FL OZ

I have had various versions of this dressing throughout the Middle East. Sometimes the ground cumin is omitted, sometimes chopped coriander or paprika are added. Serve it with egg salads, as a dressing for coleslaw salad, with warm new potatoes, or crudités.

INGREDIENTS

3–4 tsp lemon juice

6 tbsp plain yogurt

1–2 garlic cloves, finely crushed

6 tbsp olive oil

4 tbsp tahini

pinch of ground cumin

salt and freshly ground black pepper

METHOD

Whisk the lemon juice into the yogurt. Add the garlic. Slowly stir in the oil until well mixed.

Beat in the tahini then add ground cumin and seasoning to taste. Cover and chill before using.

Herby Cream Cheese Dressing

MAKES SCANT 300 ML / ½ PT

Mixing buttermilk with soft cheese makes a dressing that is creamy but not too rich. The fresh flavours of the herbs also make it taste light. Use it for cooked vegetable salads or salads containing chicken.

INGREDIENTS

115 g/4 oz full fat soft cheese

150 ml/¼ pt buttermilk

1–2 tsp lemon juice

4 tbsp chopped mixed herbs or 2 tbsp chopped tarragon or basil

salt and freshly ground black pepper

METHOD

Put the soft cheese into a bowl. Slowly pour in the buttermilk, stirring, until evenly blended. Add the lemon juice. Mix in the herbs. Season to taste. Serve chilled.

Warm Minted Lemon Cream Dressing

MAKES ABOUT 175 ML / 6 FL OZ

To make a cold dressing, simply stir all the ingredients together. This is an ideal dressing for young, sweet peas, sugar snap peas, baby carrots and baby sweetcorn.

INGREDIENTS

4 tbsp crème fraîche

finely grated rind and juice of ½ lemon

1 tbsp mint, finely chopped or shredded

75 ml/3 fl oz plain yogurt

salt and freshly ground black pepper

METHOD

Put the crème fraîche into a small saucepan and heat gently. Stir in the lemon rind and juice and the mint. When warmed through, stir in the yogurt, taking care not to let the dressing overheat. Season to taste.

Oil-free Cream Vinaigrette

MAKES ABOUT 300 ML / ½ PT

Chill the dressing well and pour it over crisp lettuce leaves, or mix with cold cooked vegetables. Do not make the dressing too far in advance otherwise the vinegar will act upon the cream and thicken it.

INGREDIENTS

½ garlic clove

salt and freshly ground white or black pepper

1 hard-boiled egg

½ tsp *Dijon* mustard

2 tsp tarragon vinegar

225 ml/8 fl oz single cream

pinch of caster sugar

METHOD

Put the garlic into a mortar or a bowl, add a pinch of salt and crush together to a paste.

Separate the egg white from the yolk; reserve the egg white for garnishing the salad. Add the egg yolk, mustard and vinegar to the bowl and mix with the garlic. Stir in the cream and add sugar and pepper to taste. Cover and chill.

RIGHT *Warm Minted Lemon Cream Dressing*

Light Herb Sauce

MAKES ABOUT 175 ML / 6 FL OZ

A simple, quick sauce that can be flavoured with any herb. If you prefer a milder dressing, leave out the shallot. Serve the dressing over green salads, warm new potato salads, vegetable salads or warm white beans such as haricot or cannelini.

INGREDIENTS

150 ml/¼ pt soured cream, Greek yogurt or plain yogurt	1 tsp shallot, finely chopped
2 tbsp herbs, chopped	salt and freshly ground white or black pepper

METHOD

Put the soured cream or yogurt, herbs and shallot into a bowl. Stir together and season to taste.

Tofu Mayonnaise

MAKES ABOUT 175 ML / 6 FL OZ

This delicious, creamy mayonnaise-style dressing is useful for vegans. It can be flavoured with a little crushed garlic, some chopped herbs or a few drops of chilli sauce. This mayonnaise can be kept in a covered container in the refrigerator for a few days.

INGREDIENTS

115 g/4 oz silken tofu	2 tbsp sunflower oil
2 tsp lemon juice	salt and freshly ground black pepper
1 tsp *Dijon* mustard	

METHOD

Put all the ingredients into a blender and mix until smooth.

Ricotta and Blue Cheese Dressing

MAKES ABOUT 425 ML / 15 FL OZ

A cheese with some piquancy is best for this dressing to contrast with the creaminess of the ricotta cheese. The dressing can be flavoured with garlic, spring onions, or herbs such as parsley, rosemary or sage. Use for warm pasta, potato, rice, butter or cannelini beans, or green lentil salads or over crisp lettuce leaves.

INGREDIENTS

150 g/5 oz ricotta cheese	150 g/5 oz crème fraîche
150 g/5 oz Stilton or other blue cheese such as Gorgonzola or Roquefort	salt and freshly ground black pepper

METHOD

Crumble the ricotta and blue cheese into a bowl and mash lightly together with a fork. Slowly pour in the crème fraîche, mixing well with a fork until the dressing is smooth. Season with a little salt and plenty of black pepper.

Creamy Mustard Vinaigrette

MAKES ABOUT 125 ML / 4½ FL OZ

Tarragon and fennel seeds give complexity to the flavour of this powerful dressing, while crème fraîche smooths the flavour with piquant creaminess. The vinaigrette is great over white bean and robust lettuce leaf salads, potato salads, cheese salads, eggs or with beef.

INGREDIENTS

¼ tsp fennel seeds	salt
1 tsp tarragon leaves	2 tbsp crème fraîche or
½ tsp *Dijon* mustard	soured cream
1½ tbsp sherry vinegar	6 tbsp olive oil

METHOD

Put the fennel seeds into a bowl and crush with the end of a rolling-pin. Add the tarragon and crush lightly.

Stir the mustard, vinegar, salt and crème fraîche into the bowl. Slowly pour in the oil, whisking until well emulsified.

Creamy Watercress Dressing

MAKES ABOUT 175 ML / 6 FL OZ

You can use all double cream or crème fraîche, or dilute either with some yogurt in whatever proportions you like, but keep at least 2 tablespoons cream or crème fraîche for some creaminess and body. Alternatively, use Greek yogurt for lightness and a creamy taste but not too many calories. Soured cream could also be used. Serve over pulse, rice or potato salads, with cold salmon, trout, chicken or eggs, or in egg sandwiches.

INGREDIENTS

large handful of watercress leaves	squeeze of lemon juice (optional)
150 ml/¼ pt double cream or crème fraîche, or a mixture of either and plain yogurt, Greek yogurt, or soured cream	salt and freshly ground white or black pepper

METHOD

Add the watercress leaves to a saucepan of boiling water and boil for 1 minute. Drain and rinse under running cold water. Drain well and dry thoroughly.

Put the watercress into a blender and add the cream, crème fraîche and/or yogurt. Mix to a green purée. Season to taste.

Yogurt and Curd Cheese "Mayonnaise"

MAKES ABOUT 150 ML / 5 FL OZ

The taste of this low-fat version of mayonnaise is not too far removed from the real thing. It can be flavoured in the same way as mayonnaise with garlic, mustard, herbs etc, and served in place of mayonnaise. A little milk can be added to thin the mayonnaise if liked.

INGREDIENTS

115 g /4 oz medium fat curd cheese or medium fat soft cheese	2 tsp olive oil
	½ tsp white wine vinegar
2 tbsp plain yogurt	salt and freshly ground black pepper

METHOD

Put the cheese into a bowl. Stir in the yogurt, oil and vinegar until smooth. Season to taste. Chill before serving.

Horseradish and Soured Cream Dressing

MAKES ABOUT 200 ML / 7 FL OZ

Spoon this dressing over sliced tomatoes, toss with boiled cauliflower for an inspired salad, or serve with sliced cold beef.

INGREDIENTS

175 ml/6 fl oz soured cream	2 tsp lemon juice or white wine vinegar
4 tbsp grated fresh or bottled horseradish	salt and freshly ground black pepper

METHOD

Pour the soured cream into a bowl. Stir in the horseradish and lemon juice or white wine vinegar to taste. Season to taste. Cover and chill.

SWEET DRESSINGS
AND MARINADES

————

Dressings and marinades can be used to quickly and easily add a special touch to fruits that are to be served for dessert. The same recipe can even sometimes double as both a marinade and a dressing (see page 93).

Spices are often included in sweet dressings and marinades because they harmonize with fruits and enhance their sweet fruitiness. Wine always makes a dish seem more luxurious. Using it as a marinade or dressing is the quickest and most simple way I know of making a dessert that I'm sure will impress, yet will be light and fresh-tasting, unlike so many "impressive" desserts which are very rich and calorie-laden.

White Wine Marinade

MAKES ABOUT 325 ML / 11 FL OZ

This is a light summery marinade that combines well with oranges, melons, peaches and pineapples. Pour it over the fruit while it is hot and leave the fruit to steep until cold.

INGREDIENTS	
300 ml/½ pt medium bodied dry white wine	long strip of lemon or lime peel
50 g/2 oz sugar	6 lemon balm leaves
	pinch of ground mace

Pour the wine into a saucepan. Add the sugar, lemon or lime peel, lemon balm leaves and mace and heat gently, stirring until the sugar has dissolved. Bring to the boil and bubble for 1 minute.

Cardamom Butter Dressing

MAKES ABOUT 200 ML / 7 FL OZ

This fragrant buttery dressing spiked with whisky or brandy adds a special air of luxury to fruit kebabs or chunks or wedges of fruit that are going to be grilled; my favourite fruits for this treatment are tropical fruits such as pineapples, mangoes, papayas, bananas, or pears. For a variation, use 2½ tablespoons finely chopped fresh ginger instead of cardamom.

INGREDIENTS	
115 g/4 oz unsalted butter, diced	2 tbsp lime or orange juice
seeds from 6 cardamom pods, crushed	2 tbsp whisky or brandy
	2 tbsp icing sugar

METHOD

Melt the butter in a small saucepan over a low heat. Stir in the remaining ingredients until evenly blended.

Strawberry Wine Marinade

MAKES ABOUT 300 ML / ½ PT

This simple but sophisticated marinade is just right for making an easy but impressive light dessert of pears, plums, peaches, apricots, cherries, lychees or mangosteens.

INGREDIENTS

4 tbsp sugar

570 ml/1 pt medium bodied dry white wine

4 large ripe strawberries

METHOD

Put the sugar and wine in a wide, shallow saucepan and heat gently, stirring until the sugar has dissolved. Bring to the boil and boil gently, without stirring, for 3–4 minutes.

Add the strawberries to the pan and simmer for 6–7 minutes until reduced by half and syrupy. Pour over the prepared fruit and leave to cool. Chill before serving.

Orange, Lemon and Honey Dressing

MAKES ABOUT 175 ML / 6 FL OZ

A favourite simple, light summer dessert is made by pouring this dressing over melon balls (preferably a combination of different melons) or cubes, orange or grapefruit slices, peaches or strawberries, then covering and chilling.

INGREDIENTS

115 ml/4 fl oz orange juice

2 tbsp lemon juice

about 2 tbsp clear honey, or to taste

METHOD

Pour the orange and lemon juices into a bowl. Add the honey and stir until melted.

Red Wine Marinade

MAKES ABOUT 375 ML / 11 FL OZ

Pour the hot marinade over sliced ripe pears, halved and pitted ripe plums, strawberries, or halved and pitted ripe peaches. If the fruit is not ripe enough to eat as it is, it can be cooked in the marinade until tender before leaving it to steep.

INGREDIENTS

300 ml/½ pt red wine

50 g/2 oz soft brown sugar

long strip of orange peel

1 tsp ground mixed spices

¼ tsp nutmeg, freshly grated

5 cm/2 in piece of cinnamon

5 cloves

METHOD

Pour the wine into a saucepan. Add the sugar, orange peel and spices and heat gently, stirring, until the sugar has dissolved. Bring to the boil and bubble for 1 minute.

Sweet Ginger, Cinnamon and Rice Wine

MAKES ABOUT 150 ML / ¼ PT MARINADE; ABOUT 40 ML / 2 FL OZ DRESSING

I use this recipe both as a marinade and a dressing for grilled fruits – first steep the fruit in it, then remove the fruit and grill it. Boil the dressing that is left until it is syrupy and brush over the hot fruit. Decorate the fruit with extra chopped crystallized ginger and serve with lime or lemon wedges.

INGREDIENTS

115 ml/4 fl oz rice wine

2 tbsp grated fresh ginger

1 tbsp finely chopped crystallized ginger

½ cinnamon stick

pinch of sugar

METHOD

Put all the ingredients into a small saucepan and bring just to boiling point. Pour over the fruit and leave to cool. Using a slotted spoon, scoop out the fruit. Strain the marinade into a small saucepan and boil until syrupy.

Grill the fruit until lightly browned then pour over the ginger and rice wine syrup.

Spiced Citrus Syrup

MAKES ABOUT 450 ML / 16 FL OZ

This syrup is for pouring over fruit salads, and is particularly good with tropical fruits such as mangoes and papayas, melons, oranges, pears and grapes.

INGREDIENTS

300 ml/½ pt water

115 g/4 oz sugar

2 large strips of lime or lemon rind

2 large strips of orange rind

½ tsp ground ginger

1 cinnamon stick

lime or lemon juice to taste

METHOD

Pour the water into a saucepan, add the sugar and heat gently, stirring until the sugar has dissolved. Add the fruit rinds, ginger and cinnamon and bring slowly to the boil. Remove from the heat, cover and leave until cold. Chill.

Before using, strain the syrup and add lime or lemon juice to taste.

Ginger Dressing

MAKES ABOUT 350 ML / 12 FL OZ

Tropical fruit salads, containing, for example, lychees, mangoes, pineapple or papaya, oranges, clementines and tangerines, grapefruits and pears marry particularly well with this dressing.

INGREDIENTS

50 g/2 oz caster sugar

150 ml/¼ pt water

150 ml/¼ pt ginger wine

2 pieces stem ginger preserved in syrup, finely chopped

finely grated zest and juice of 1½ limes

METHOD

Put the sugar and water into a saucepan and heat gently, stirring, until the sugar has dissolved. Bring to the boil then simmer for 1 minute without stirring. Remove the pan from the heat and add the ginger wine, chopped stem ginger and lime zest and juice.

Pour over the prepared fruit and leave to cool. Chill before serving.

8

MARINADES
AND SPICE RUBS

Marinades can be simple or complex, or anywhere between the two. They can be light with just a light flavour, or they can be richly flavoured with exotic spices from many different cuisines around the world.

Whatever ingredients you are using, including the oils, herbs and spices, make sure they are fresh because even a slight stale or off flavour will penetrate the food to be marinated, so spoiling it.

The flavour of marinades will improve if they are left to stand for 30 minutes or more. Marinades can be made in advance and kept in an airtight container in the refrigerator for a few days.

Herb Marinade

MAKES ABOUT 150 ML / 5 FL OZ

This is a universal, versatile marinade that can be used for meat, poultry, fish or vegetables. Be sure to use a well-flavoured olive oil. The herbs can be varied according to the food that is to be marinated and what is available.

INGREDIENTS

4 tbsp olive oil

2 tbsp lemon or lime juice or white wine vinegar

1 garlic clove, crushed and finely chopped

4 tbsp chopped fres herbs

freshly ground black pepper

METHOD

Mix all the ingredients together.

Orange and Herb Marinade

MAKES ABOUT 300 ML / 10 FL OZ

White wine adds a special flavour to this marinade and therefore the foods marinated in it. I use it for pork, chicken, poussins, duck and lamb.

INGREDIENTS

juice of 2 oranges

150 ml/¼ pt dry white wine

3 tbsp olive oil

1 tsp chopped marjoram

1 tsp chopped thyme

1 tsp chopped rosemary

1 garlic clove, crushed

freshly ground black pepper

METHOD

Put all the ingredients into a bowl and whisk together.

Yogurt and Chilli Marinade

MAKES ABOUT 175 ML / 6 FL OZ

I use this marinade to spread over shelled large prawns before grilling them. It can also be used for chicken kebabs.

INGREDIENTS

115 ml/4 fl oz plain yogurt

1 onion, finely chopped

2 garlic cloves

2 fresh red chillies, deseeded and chopped

juice of 1 lime

chilli powder (optional)

salt and freshly ground black pepper

METHOD

Put the yogurt, onion, garlic, chillies and lime juice in a blender. Mix to a paste. Add chilli powder if liked, and season to taste.

Marinade for Grilled Vegetables

MAKES ABOUT 175 ML / 6 FL OZ

Steep the grilled vegetables in this marinade, overnight at room temperature then serve as an anti-pasta, a first course accompanied by good, firm bread to mop up the juices, or as part of a buffet.

INGREDIENTS

8 tbsp olive oil

1 tbsp sherry vinegar

1 garlic clove, finely crushed

1 shallot, finely chopped

1 fresh red chilli, deseeded and finely chopped

salt and freshly ground black pepper

METHOD

Put all the ingredients into a bowl and mix together.

Souvlakia Marinade

MAKES ABOUT 150 ML / 5 FL OZ

Souvlakia, tasty grilled or barbecued lamb kebabs that are usually served with yogurt trickled over, in split pitta breads, are sold throughout Greece by street vendors, cafés and restaurants.

INGREDIENTS

4 garlic cloves

1 onion

1 tsp ground cumin

1 tsp cayenne pepper or a few drops of Tabasco sauce

50 ml/2 fl oz olive oil

freshly ground black pepper

METHOD

Put the garlic and onion into a blender, add the spices and oil and mix until reduced to a slush. Season with black pepper.

RIGHT *Marinade for Grilled Vegetables*

Mandarin Marinade

MAKES ABOUT 225 ML / 8 FL OZ

This slightly sweet, yet sharp, citrus flavoured marinade spiked with fresh ginger can be used with beef, lamb, pork, wild and reared duck and pigeon.

INGREDIENTS

2 tbsp mandarin or orange marmalade	50 ml/2 fl oz orange juice
1 tsp fresh ginger, grated	50 ml/2 fl oz lemon juice
1 garlic clove, crushed	115 ml/4 fl oz olive oil
50 ml/2 fl oz white wine vinegar	freshly ground black pepper

METHOD

Put all the ingredients except the oil and seasoning in a saucepan and heat, stirring, until the marmalade has melted. Simmer until reduced to 150 ml/4 fl oz. Pour into a bowl and leave to cool.

Stir in the oil and season with black pepper to taste.

Lime and Pernod Marinade

MAKES ABOUT 225 ML / 8 FL. OZ.

Lime marries well with the anise flavour of Pernod to make a marinade that is ideal for seafood, especially large, raw prawns and scallops and thick pieces of fresh haddock.

INGREDIENTS

4 tbsp Pernod

juice of 2 limes

1 small garlic clove, crushed (optional)

1 tsp fennel seeds, lightly crushed

1½ tbsp chopped coriander

75 ml/3 fl oz olive oil

freshly ground black pepper

METHOD

Put all the ingredients into a bowl and stir together.

Coriander, Lime and Vermouth Marinade

MAKES ABOUT 175 ML / 6 FL OZ

Dry white vermouths are flavoured with blends of herbs and spices. As each producer has their own special blend, the taste (and quality) of vermouths varies between brands. If you would like to add a bit of "heat", add a drop or two of Tabasco sauce.

INGREDIENTS

3 tbsp chopped coriander

finely grated rind and juice of 2 limes

2 tbsp dry white vermouth

2 garlic cloves, crushed

50 ml/2 fl oz olive oil

Tabasco sauce (optional)

freshly ground black pepper

METHOD

Put all the ingredients into a bowl and mix together.

Salmoriglio

MAKES ABOUT 300 ML / ½ PT

In Sicily, salmoriglio is used as the marinade for fish that is to be grilled or barbecued, usually threaded onto skewers. Sicilians believe that the only way to make a really good salmoriglio is to add seawater; in the absence of this ingredient use sea salt for seasoning. Salmoriglio can also be served warm as a sauce to accompany the fish.

INGREDIENTS

1 garlic clove	175 ml/6 fl oz virgin olive oil, warmed slightly
1 tbsp finely chopped parsley	3 tbsp hot water
1½ tsp chopped oregano	about 4 tbsp lemon juice
about 1 tsp rosemary, chopped	sea salt and freshly ground black pepper

METHOD

Put the garlic, the herbs and a pinch of salt into a mortar or bowl and pound to a paste with a pestle or the end of a rolling pin.

Pour the oil into a warm bowl then, using a fork, slowly pour in the hot water followed by the lemon juice, whisking constantly until well emulsified. Add the herb and garlic mixture, and black pepper to taste.

Put the bowl over a saucepan of hot water and warm for 5 minutes, whisking occasionally. Leave to cool before using.

Yogurt and Sun-dried Tomato Marinade

MAKES ABOUT 175 ML / 6 FL OZ

This is a very simple yet effective marinade to spread over salmon, trout or chicken. Ground spices such as cumin and cardamom can be added for a spicy flavour, if liked.

INGREDIENTS

150 g/5 oz plain yogurt	1 tbsp lemon juice
1 large garlic clove, crushed	1 tbsp sun-dried tomato paste
finely grated zest of 1 lemon	freshly ground black pepper

METHOD

Put the yogurt into a bowl. Add the remaining ingredients and stir together.

LEFT *Salmoriglio*

Orange and Honey Marinade

MAKES ABOUT 450 ML / 16 FL OZ

A simple but very effective marinade for barbecued spare ribs; it also works well with pork chops and steaks.

INGREDIENTS

300 ml/½ pt pure orange juice from a carton

3 tbsp clear honey

2 tbsp lemon juice

1 tbsp soy sauce

3 tbsp Worcestershire sauce

METHOD

Pour the orange juice into a saucepan, add the honey and heat gently, stirring, until the honey has dissolved.

Remove from the heat, add the remaining ingredients and leave to cool.

Orange and Ginger Marinade

MAKES ABOUT 400 ML / 14 FL OZ

Soy sauce adds depth and richness to the orange juice, lemon juice adds a tang and grated fresh ginger gives a zesty flavour, all of which combine to make this an ideal marinade for giving distinction to chicken, duck, turkey and pork.

INGREDIENTS

200 ml/7 fl oz orange juice

4 tbsp lemon juice

1 tbsp fresh ginger, grated

4 tbsp light soy sauce

1 tbsp white wine vinegar

4 tbsp dry sherry

1 plump garlic clove, crushed

freshly ground black pepper

METHOD

Put all the ingredients into a bowl and whisk together.

Dried Apricot Marinade

MAKES ABOUT 225 ML / 8 FL OZ

Curry powder adds an appetizing spicy note to the deep fruit flavour of dried apricots to make a marinade that transforms lamb, whole chicken or chicken portions with skin, pork or duck.

INGREDIENTS

115 g/4 oz dried apricots, soaked overnight

2 tbsp olive oil

1 large onion, sliced

1 garlic clove, finely chopped

1½ tsp curry powder

1½ tbsp white wine vinegar

1½ tbsp lemon juice

pinch of cayenne pepper

1½ tsp sugar

freshly ground black pepper

METHOD

Put the apricots into a small saucepan and add enough of their soaking liquid to just cover. Bring to the boil then simmer gently for 15–20 minutes or until tender.

Allow to cool slightly, tip into a blender and mix to a purée.

Heat the oil in a frying pan, add the onion and garlic and fry until softened and golden. Stir in the curry powder for 1 minute then add the apricot purée and remaining ingredients. Stir well. Bring to the boil then leave to cool.

Coconut Marinade

MAKES ABOUT 225 ML / 8 FL OZ

This Far-Eastern style marinade works well with firm fish such as monkfish, or with chicken, turkey, pork or lamb.

INGREDIENTS

150 ml/¼ pt boiling water

75 g/3 oz creamed coconut block, chopped

1 tsp lime juice

1 shallot, finely chopped

1 garlic clove, finely chopped

1 lemon grass stalk, thoroughly crushed

the seeds from 3 cardamom pods, crushed

1.25 cm/½ in piece of fresh ginger, grated

½ tsp ground cumin

freshly ground black pepper

METHOD

Pour the boiling water over the coconut and stir until smooth. Add the remaining ingredients and cool.

Green Peppercorn, Mustard and Parsley Marinade

MAKES ABOUT 225 ML / 8 FL OZ

A spicy mustard paste to spread thickly over thick lamb steaks and lamb chops to give them a real lift.

INGREDIENTS

1 tbsp green peppercorns, finely chopped

4 tbsp wholegrain mustard

3 tbsp white and green parts of spring onions

25 g/1 oz fresh breadcrumbs

3 tbsp parsley, chopped

¼ tsp cayenne pepper

1 tbsp corn oil

METHOD

Put the peppercorns, mustard, spring onions, breadcrumbs, parsley and cayenne pepper into a bowl and stir together thoroughly. Stir in the oil a drop at a time to make a thick paste.

Yogurt and Mint Marinade

MAKES ABOUT 115 ML / 4 FL OZ

Mint is married to lamb in the Middle East as well as in England. Here it is combined with thick, creamy yogurt to produce meltingly tender lamb kebabs, grilled lamb chops and steaks and roast lamb. The marinade also works well with chicken and turkey.

INGREDIENTS

6 tbsp Greek yogurt

1 garlic clove, crushed

about 2 tbsp chopped mint

freshly ground black pepper

METHOD

Stir all the ingredients together.

Spiced Yogurt Marinade

MAKES ABOUT 175 ML / 6 FL OZ

This is one of my favourite marinades to use for chicken drumsticks and thighs that are to be grilled, or, better still, barbecued. It can also be used for fish or lamb.

INGREDIENTS

150 ml/¼ pt plain yogurt	2 tsp paprika pepper
2 garlic cloves	½ tsp ground chilli
1 tbsp fresh ginger, chopped	½ tsp ground cardamom
1 tbsp ground cumin	

METHOD

Put all the ingredients into a blender and mix together until smooth.

Yogurt and Herb Marinade

MAKES ABOUT 200 ML / 7 FL OZ

The herbs can be varied depending on which type of meat or poultry is being used, for example tarragon, thyme, sage or lemon balm go with chicken; rosemary, tarragon, thyme or mint with lamb; rosemary or parsley with beef; sage or bay with pork.

INGREDIENTS

4 tbsp olive oil	2 garlic cloves, crushed
150 ml/¼ pt plain yogurt	freshly ground black pepper
about 4 tbsp chopped fresh herbs	

METHOD

Put all the ingredients into a bowl and mix together.

ABOVE *Spiced Yogurt Marinade*

Apple, Lemon and Ginger Marinade

MAKES ABOUT 175 ML / 6 FL OZ

This tangy, fruity dressing makes a good marriage with chicken, turkey, duck or pork.

INGREDIENTS

6 tbsp unsweetened apple juice

3 lemon slices, finely chopped

2 cm/¾ in piece of fresh ginger, grated

1 garlic clove, crushed

3 tbsp dry sherry

3 tbsp soy sauce

METHOD

Put all the ingredients into a bowl and mix together.

Sherry, Soy, Ginger, Coriander and Star Anise Marinade

MAKES ABOUT 350 ML / 12 FL OZ

When I want to give a change from plain roast lamb, pork or beef, I marinate the joint in this recipe; the subtle, complex flavours give the meat a really special taste. I have also used the marinade for mature pheasants that are to be casseroled or braised.

INGREDIENTS

150 ml/5 fl oz dry or medium sherry

150 ml/5 fl oz soy sauce

2.5 cm/1 in piece of fresh ginger, grated

4 garlic cloves, crushed

2 tbsp coriander, chopped

2 tbsp clear honey

3 star anise, lightly crushed

METHOD

Put all the ingredients into a bowl and mix together.

Tandoori Marinade

MAKES ABOUT 450 ML / 16 FL OZ

This is an authentic-tasting tandoori marinade for skinned chicken portions, cubes of lamb, raw jumbo prawns peeled but with the heads left on, or firm-fleshed fish.

INGREDIENTS

1 onion, coarsely chopped

4 large garlic cloves

25 g/1 oz fresh ginger

4 tbsp lemon juice

225 ml/8 fl oz plain yogurt

4 tbsp sunflower oil

1 tbsp ground turmeric

1 tbsp ground coriander

1 tsp ground cumin

½ tsp ground cinnamon

½ tsp grated nutmeg

½ tsp freshly ground black pepper

¼ tsp ground cloves

¼ tsp ground chillies or cayenne pepper

METHOD

Put the onion, garlic and ginger into a blender and process until chopped. Add the remaining ingredients and mix until smooth.

Thai-style Marinade

MAKES ABOUT 175 ML / 6 FL OZ

Here, typical ingredients of the Thai cuisine produce a well-flavoured marinade that I have used with great success for grilled tuna, salmon or swordfish steaks, firm white fish such as monkfish and cod, and chicken.

INGREDIENTS

2 garlic cloves, crushed

1 fresh green chilli, deseeded and finely chopped

2 tbsp chopped coriander

2 tbsp chopped basil

2 tbsp chopped mint

1.25 cm/½ in piece of fresh ginger, grated

50 ml/2 fl oz lime juice

1 tbsp fish sauce

1 tbsp sesame oil

freshly ground black pepper

METHOD

Put all the ingredients into a bowl. Stir together until well mixed.

Hoisin Sauce Marinade

MAKES ABOUT 175 ML / 6 FL OZ

Hoisin sauce is a thick, slightly sweet, smooth Chinese bean sauce with a mild garlic taste. It is now widely available in supermarkets as well as Chinese grocers. Used in this recipe, hoisin sauce makes a marinade that adds a touch of distinction to bland meat such as modern battery-reared chicken and mass-produced pork without overpowering it.

INGREDIENTS

6 tbsp hoisin sauce	2 tsp chopped thyme
4 tbsp rice wine	freshly ground black pepper
2 tbsp olive oil	

METHOD

Put all the ingredients into a bowl. Stir together.

Spiced Sesame Oil Marinade

MAKES ABOUT 115 ML / 4 FL OZ

You will get quite different results whether you use lime or lemon juice. Either way, this marinade is good for pork, chicken, fish or shellfish.

INGREDIENTS

1 plump garlic clove, finely chopped	1 tbsp sesame oil
2 spring onions, finely chopped	2 tbsp groundnut oil
1.25 cm/½ in of fresh ginger, grated	2 tbsp sake or dry sherry
	1 tbsp lemon or lime juice

METHOD

Put all the ingredients into a bowl. Whisk together.

Golden Escabeche Marinade

MAKES ABOUT 350 ML / 12 FL OZ

The name "escabeche" is derived from the Perso-Arabic word "sikbaj" which means "vinegar stew" and is applied, particularly in Spain and Mexico, to dishes of meat, poultry, game or fish that are cooked then steeped in an acid-based marinade to help extend their edible shelf-life. With modern freezing and refrigeration techniques this practice is no longer necessary but escabeche dishes are so good to eat that they are still prepared. This is my all-time favourite escabeche marinade.

INGREDIENTS

large pinch of saffron strands

3 tbsp medium bodied dry white wine, or hot water

2 tbsp virgin olive oil

2 red onions, thinly sliced

1½ tsp cumin seeds, lightly crushed

½ tsp dried chilli flakes

2 red peppers, sliced

finely grated rind and juice of 1 orange

juice of 1 lemon

pinch of sugar

salt and freshly ground black pepper

METHOD

Soak the saffron strands in the wine or water for 5 minutes.

Heat the olive oil in a frying pan, add the onions and cook for 2 minutes. Stir in the cumin seeds and chilli flakes for about 45 seconds then add the red peppers. Fry, stirring occasionally, until soft. Add the saffron liquid, orange rind and juice and the lemon juice. Bubble for a few minutes then add sugar and seasoning to taste. Leave to cool.

Curry Marinade

MAKES ABOUT 200 ML / 7 FL OZ

Add an appetizing curry flavour to grilled chicken and turkey with this marinade. The strength of the curry flavour can be adjusted by altering the amount of curry powder or garam masala that is added, or using a hotter curry powder.

INGREDIENTS

75 ml/3 fl oz white wine vinegar

115 ml/4 fl oz olive oil

1 garlic clove, crushed

1 tsp curry powder or garam masala

freshly ground black pepper

METHOD

Put all the ingredients into a bowl and whisk together.

RIGHT *Golden Escabeche Marinade*

Saffron and Lemon Marinade

MAKES ABOUT 175 ML / 6 FL OZ

Saffron and lemon combine to make an elegant marinade that originated in Italy. It is used for courgettes and large prawns, but is also worth trying with scallops, firm white fish or chicken breasts. Two tablespoons of chopped capers can be added for an additional piquant flavour.

INGREDIENTS

pinch of saffron threads

1 tbsp hot water

2 garlic cloves, finely crushed

juice of 1½ lemons

2 tbsp white wine vinegar

130 ml/4½ fl oz mild olive oil

freshly ground black pepper

METHOD

Put the saffron in a bowl, pour over the water and leave to steep for 5 minutes. Add the remaining ingredients. Whisk together.

Fennel Marinade

MAKES ABOUT 115 ML / 4 FL OZ

The fresh aniseed flavour of fennel works particularly well with pork and is also effective with rabbit and chicken.

INGREDIENTS

1 garlic clove	4 tbsp fennel leaves, chopped
seeds from 1 star anise	2 tbsp olive oil

METHOD

Put the garlic and star anise seeds into a mortar or bowl and crush together with a pestle or the end of a rolling-pin. Add the fennel leaves, crush these a few times, then trickle in the oil, crushing to make a paste.

Satay Marinade

MAKES ABOUT 115 ML / 4 FL OZ

Satays are ubiquitous throughout South East Asia so you will find many different recipes for satays themselves and for the marinades and sauces that accompany them. This is one of my favourite satay marinades that I use for satays of pork, chicken or large prawns. Serve with Indonesian Peanut Dressing (see page 51).

INGREDIENTS

4 tbsp coconut milk	2 tsp ground coriander
1 tbsp soft dark brown sugar	2 tsp ground cumin
1 garlic clove, finely chopped	1 tsp ground turmeric
	squeeze of lemon juice

METHOD

Mix all the ingredients together to make a fairly dry paste. Spoon over the ingredients to be marinated and rub the marinade thoroughly over them.

White Wine Marinade

MAKES ABOUT 300 ML / ½ PT

Lighter than a red wine marinade, this recipe is suitable for farmed pigeon and rabbit, young partridge and pheasant, lamb, and chicken, turkey and pork when you want a more robust dish.

INGREDIENTS

2 tbsp mild olive oil

1 shallot, finely chopped

1 carrot, finely chopped

2 juniper berries, crushed

2 black peppercorns, crushed

1 sprig of celery leaves, chopped

2 parsley stalks

1 bay leaf, torn

1 sprig of thyme

1 slice of lemon

about 300 ml/½ pt medium bodied dry white wine

METHOD

Put all the ingredients into a bowl and stir. If the meat is not covered by the marinade, add some more wine.

Devilled Marinade

MAKES ABOUT 175 ML / 6 FL OZ

The use of the name "devilled" indicates that it is highly seasoned with a hot ingredient such as mustard. Spread onto chicken portions with skin, turkey, lamb or beef.

INGREDIENTS

4 tbsp tomato ketchup

1 tbsp lemon juice

1 tbsp paprika pepper

4 tsp ground cumin

4 tsp ground turmeric

1 tbsp English mustard powder

50 g/2 oz unsalted butter, chopped

METHOD

Put the tomato ketchup and lemon juice into a bowl. Stir in the paprika, cumin, turmeric and mustard powder.

Put the butter into a small saucepan and heat gently until just melted. Stir the butter into the spice mixture until evenly combined.

Mexican Marinade

MAKES ABOUT 150 ML / 5 FL OZ

A hot and lightly spicy marinade that is most suitable for pork, but also can be used for chicken, turkey, lamb or beef.

INGREDIENTS

2 garlic cloves, finely crushed

2 fresh red or green chillies, deseeded and chopped

¼ tsp dried thyme

¼ tsp ground cumin

pinch of ground cloves

75 ml/3 fl oz white wine vinegar

freshly ground black pepper

METHOD

Put all the ingredients into a bowl and stir together.

Cooked Red Wine Marinade

MAKES 350 ML / 12 FL OZ

Simmering the vegetables, spices and herbs in the wine mellows their flavours and draws them into the wine (which is also concentrated by the simmering), so giving a marinade that has a richer, more well-rounded flavour than an uncooked marinade.

INGREDIENTS

50 ml/2 fl oz olive oil	50 ml/2 fl oz red wine vinegar
1 small onion, chopped	
2 garlic cloves, chopped	6 juniper berries, crushed
	6 black peppercorns, crushed
1 celery stick, chopped	
400 ml/14 fl oz medium bodied red wine	1 bouquet garni

METHOD

Heat half the oil in a saucepan, add the onion, garlic, carrot and celery and fry until soft but not browned. Add the wine, wine vinegar, juniper berries, peppercorns and bouquet garni. Bring to the boil then simmer for 15–20 minutes until the vegetables are tender. Add the remaining oil, cover and leave to cool.

Uncooked Spiced Red Wine Marinade

MAKES ABOUT 300 ML / ½ PT

This marinade is quite sweet. Use it to flavour and tenderize beef, lamb or pork.

INGREDIENTS

1 tsp coriander seeds

1 tsp cumin seeds

1–2 garlic cloves, crushed

1 small onion, finely chopped

½ tsp dried chilli flakes

1 tbsp soft brown sugar

5 tbsp red wine

115 ml/4 fl oz olive oil

METHOD

Heat the coriander and cumin seeds in a small heavy frying pan and fry until fragrant, shaking the pan.

Pour into a bowl and add the remaining ingredients.

Uncooked Red Wine Marinade

MAKES ABOUT 350 ML / 12 FL OZ

Well-flavoured with vegetables, spices and herbs and boosted with port, this marinade produces tasty beef, young hare and venison, wild pigeon and pheasant dishes.

INGREDIENTS

2 tbsp olive oil

1 onion, finely chopped

2 garlic cloves, crushed

2 carrots, finely chopped

1 stick of celery, finely chopped

6 juniper berries, crushed

8 black peppercorns, crushed

2–3 parsley stalks

2 sprigs of thyme

2 bay leaves, torn

1 sprig of rosemary

115 ml/4 fl oz port

about 225 ml/8 fl oz red wine, or enough to cover meat

METHOD

Put all the ingredients into a bowl and mix together. If the meat is not covered by the marinade, add some more red wine.

Spice Rub for Meat

MAKES ABOUT 7 TBSP

I use this spice rub for beef, pork and lamb.

INGREDIENTS

1 tsp oregano, finely chopped

1 tsp fennel seeds, crushed

½ small garlic clove, finely chopped

1 tbsp paprika pepper

½ tsp cayenne pepper

freshly ground black pepper

METHOD

Put all the ingredients into a bowl and mix together.

Garlicky Spice Rub

MAKES ABOUT 5 TBSP

This spice rub is especially effective with lamb and pork but can also be enjoyed with chicken and turkey.

INGREDIENTS

1 tsp dried thyme

4 garlic cloves, finely chopped

1 dried bay leaf, crushed

6 black peppercorns, crushed

METHOD

Put all the ingredients into a bowl and mix together.

Cajun Spice Rub

MAKES ABOUT 7 TBSP

In addition to dried herbs and ground cumin, this spice rub also contains onion and garlic. It is especially effective with red meats. Dried basil, sage or fennel can be substituted for the dried thyme or oregano for a change.

INGREDIENTS

1 plump garlic clove	½ tsp ground cumin
½ small onion, chopped	½ tsp mustard powder
1 tsp dried thyme	½ tsp freshly ground
1 tsp dried oregano	black pepper

METHOD

Put the garlic and onion into a mortar or small bowl and crush with a pestle or the end of a rolling-pin. Mix in the remaining ingredients.

Spice Rub for Fish

MAKES ABOUT 9 TBSP

The lemon, tarragon and basil in this recipe make it particularly suitable for fish.

INGREDIENTS

2 tsp lemon rind, finely grated

1 tsp dried tarragon, finely chopped

1 tsp dried basil, chopped

½ small garlic clove, finely chopped

1 tbsp paprika pepper

½ tsp cayenne pepper

freshly ground black pepper

METHOD

Put all the ingredients into a bowl and stir together.

Simple Spice Rub

MAKES ABOUT 3 TBSP

I like to use this simple spice rub only for large pieces of salmon or tuna.

INGREDIENTS

1 tsp cumin seeds	seeds from 6 cardamom pods
1 tsp coriander seeds	½ tsp black peppercorns

METHOD

Heat a dry, small, heavy frying pan, add all the seeds and heat until fragrant, shaking the pan frequently.

Tip the spices into a small blender, a spice grinder, mortar or a bowl. Grind finely, or crush finely with the end of a rolling-pin.

Spice Rub for Chicken and Turkey

MAKES ABOUT 7 TBSP

Being particularly herby, this spice rub really perks up chicken and turkey.

INGREDIENTS

1 tsp dried tarragon, finely chopped	½ small garlic clove, finely chopped
¾ tsp dried marjoram, finely chopped	1 tbsp paprika pepper
¼ tsp dried thyme, finely chopped	½ tsp cayenne pepper
¼ tsp dried sage, finely chopped	freshly ground black pepper

METHOD

Put all the ingredients into a bowl and mix together.